THE

Debriefing of Markus Burns

MARKUS BURNS

THE DEBRIEFING OF MARKUS BURNS. Copyright July 2020 by Markus Burns. All rights reserved. No part of this publication may be reproduced, distributed, or transmitted in any form or by any means, including photocopying, recording, or other electronic or mechanical methods, without the prior written permission of the publisher, except in the case of brief quotations embodied in critical reviews and certain other noncommercial uses permitted by copyright law.

For permission requests, write to the publisher, addressed "Attention: Permissions Coordinator," 205 N. Michigan Avenue, Suite #810, Chicago, IL 60601. 13th & Joan books may be purchased for educational, business or sales promotional use. For information, please email the Sales Department at sales@13thandjoan.com.

Printed in the U. S. A.

First Printing, December 2020

Library of Congress Cataloging-in-Publication Data has been applied for.

ISBN: 978-1-953156-13-6

Dedication

THIS BOOK IS dedicated to those who have struggled, lost their way, and their faith. I pen this book giving a voice to those who have experienced feeling unloved and lacking guidance. I speak through this narrative to those who don't remember the last time they felt safe nor protected. I encourage those on the path to beating the odds. You, my friends, are part of my tribe. The hopeless and the helpless is the voice that gave rise to this work. I have been in those shoes. Although I found my way out of poverty; I know there are many like me. Moreover, I hope my story gives you the strength to strive until you thrive. The life you dream of is waiting for you to survive your test! If you are reading this and you currently feel like your life is a mess or things are spiraling, I encourage you to pray. Please realize that no one is coming to save you but you. Take five minutes to pity yourself. Yes, that is all the time you can pity yourself. Now, it is time to start thinking. It is time to unlearn and relearn what is needed to be successful. I hope to inspire you enough to make the life you want to manifest happen for you. Remember, life is about keeping it pushing no matter what!

Introduction

DUE TO THE coronavirus pandemic, many industries in the world closed. Some closed temporarily, while others, on the other hand, closed permanently. I finally got a moment to shut down. I had an opportunity to close myself off from my typical daily experience. I was able to shut down some of the many thoughts and quiet my inner voice to finally breathe, recalibrate, and like so many others, examine what is important to me. I was able to experience much-needed quiet time.

    I was talking to a friend and we were discussing how everything that's happening is changing how we see life. Both of us agreed that we could no longer continue postponing the things we wanted to do for ourselves and others. That's when I realized that it was time to write this book. Almost everyone that knows pieces of my story tells me I should write a book. I made two other attempts before, but I never finished. After that, I promised myself that I wouldn't make another attempt until I've done something worthy in my life. So here I am, feeling worthy and somewhat accomplished. Working in the television production industry, I have been telling other people's stories for the last five years. I witness firsthand how powerful it is to share your truth with someone else. Honestly, you can change someone's life just by letting them know they are not alone in a situation. That's what I want to do. I want to share my story to open eyes and hopefully display some meaningful wisdom. So here I am, wanting to be on the streets with the protesters, but I know that what I am doing right now is my part in the movement. I was told by a friend that I am a lightworker. I'm not totally sure if that's true, but I hope that this book shines some light in someone's life. Also, I think it's more important that as a Black man, I control my narrative. People need to know who I really am, and who better to tell that than me?

I am a representation of many of the young kids who live in the projects or poor communities and grow up facing countless obstacles. I'm just one of the lucky kids who survived and got the opportunity to live long enough to be an adult. I feel that if people in the world understood that the little Black boy, you're looking at, projecting nothing but negative thoughts towards is just a product of the environment, one which a lot of powerful people purposely created. The reality is just like everyone else, we need someone with resources who's genuinely concerned about us, and cares enough to stay by our side until we are in a better place. That's what changed things for me so that's what I believe.

Some of the topics I'm writing about are not going to be easy. I learned a while ago that I gained the life skills of a survivor. I learned how to compartmentalize things and avoid the immediate pain of a situation just by focusing on the reality of what needs to happen in order for me to live. When I say live, I mean that in every sense of the word. Living is a main priority for all of us; the difference is that living looks different to all of us. Although I was walking and breathing, I never looked at myself as living until I was able to happily be effective in the life of my loved ones. Thinking about the roads I have traveled in my lifetime often leaves me a bit shocked. At times

I had to check myself to make sure I wasn't lying to myself. There have been days I've called my older brother and sister just to cross reference situations I remember. I found out that my memory is just as good as I imagined. The situations you will read about are situations that made me who I am. I have come to embrace the path I walked on. Now, I don't wish my path on anyone else. I know life isn't fair and only strong people can accept that and keep it pushing, in my opinion. The crazy thing is right now outside there is a mass of strong people who realize how unfair life is and they aren't taking no for an answer. What a beautiful thing to see! This pandemic is a gift for some and a curse for others. So far, it's giving me something I needed: a moment of clarity.

Acknowledgements

TO MY SIBLINGS: Jamour, Kim, Nikki, Nathan, and Nyia, there's a part of each and every one of you inside of me. I love you all. To my daughter, Alana, I got you no matter what may come. To my mother, thank you for making me strong. I love you. Aunt Faith and Uncle Crowder, thank you for providing me with stability and normalcy when I needed it. Uncle Crowder, you taught me to be a man. To my best friend, Glad (Esther Shucks), Turina, Ashley, Porsha, Whitney, and Maine, thank you for never changing or turning your back on me. Yomi Martin, the first person to ever put 2K in my hand to support my dream. Dana Christian, for teaching me how to work a camera and introducing me to everyone in your circle. Marilyn Gill, because you embraced me, my life changed. Joye Chin, you are a lightworker and heaven-sent. Angel Johnson, Shawn Baker, Debbie Carter. Carlos King, you taught me well when it comes to producing. Aunt Vivian, Uncle Jackie, Aunt Janie, Aunt Lessie, Aunt Naomi, Uncle Nathan, Aunt Debra, thank you. Uncle Gene, I miss you! Yvonne and Rod, thank you guys for always being there for me. You all have in one way or another contributed to the person I am today. Tequilla Broussard thank you for my child. Omar Burns, my close friend and older cousin Davanthony Conners thank you. To my fiancée Alexus Casey, I pray we last until it's lights out! James Smith, Raymond Rhodes, Terrance Redd Claiborne, Rodney Breedlove, Rod Rose, Darnell Hood, Chazz Brogden, Lauren Eskelin, Lorraine Haughton and the team at Truly Orignal (thank you for the support you have given throughout these years). All my cousins, I love you all!

To all my nieces and nephews: Ananda, Allen, Elijah, Kelly, Kristin, Andrea, Donte, Neyah, Jamour, Jaylen, Cam, Royal, and Nyla I am her for you and love you!

Nasir Jones, through your music I learned how to think and see clearly while moving through the neighborhoods.

Grandma, I miss you every day. Thank you for being my angel.

All of you who have ever come in my life and made an impact, I thank you because you played your part in making me who I am today.

To the reader of this book, I need you to believe! That is the main mission of this book. As a Black man in America, believing in yourself is a superpower. It's a superpower because, we, as Black men, are reminded daily of how the world views us. We live in a land where we must show up for ourselves. Whether it is the media showing a negative news report, a defaming article, a rap song on the radio paying homage to a fallen friend, or a family member telling me to be safe anytime I leave out the door as a Black man, I must enter the world knowing I have not only what it takes to survive, but also knowing that I will thrive.

They don't have to go into detail about being safe. I know what they mean. I grew up keenly aware of my circumstances. A hard life was expected. I thought my way of living was normal, until I started learning about my history. Not my history regarding slavery, but the history between America and African Americans after we were added to the constitution. Once I realized that I was hated and targeted, and my circumstances weren't deemed by God but created by someone who saw me as an enemy, I was highly offended. How is it possible to thrive in an atmosphere of hate? I have chosen to redefine myself based on my knowledge. I don't see myself the way many people see us, as Blacks. Additionally, my heart and my pride will not allow me to accept this position as I live. By the end of this book, you will see how deeply I believe that I was destined to rise above the standards America has set for Black people. Furthermore, you will grow to understand that you too are destined to rise above the low standards America insists on reinforcing on us as a people. I believe in you! Now it's up to you to believe in you!

Racism and hate have no discretion. The systems that are in place for us to fail don't regard the fact that we become victims of this as children.

I have learned that many of my experiences are foreign to my White counterparts. I didn't have a father, therefore I sought advice from other, older men. Initially, I did not care if they were Black or White. I remember asking an older White guy for fatherly advice, unfortunately, I was met with disgust. It was a harsh reality to face but a lesson learned.

In this book I am giving you a glimpse into my life. The harsh circumstances I encountered with my family as an adolescent, moments of my life as a teenager on my own, trying to find myself and father my child. I'm transparent with my moments of insecurities. America consistently strives to invalidate our feelings as a people. Systemic racism perpetuates the inaccurate notion that Black people are inferior. Trust me, we are not, and we hurt; we often hurt alone in silence, accepting the neglect of our past, trying to live by the standards of an American man.

TABLE OF Contents

ONE | Dear America 15
TWO | Hello 19
THREE | Welcome to My Broken Home 29
FOUR | Trying to Understand 35
FIVE | Limited Guidance 45
SIX | Evicted 49
SEVEN | Memphis 53
EIGHT | Label Me a Runaway 63
NINE | Journey for Peace and Love 67
TEN | My Role Model 75
ELEVEN | Milwaukee 93
TWELVE | Roads Traveled 109
THIRTEEN | To the Younger Me 125
FOURTEEN | Realizing My Purpose 127
FIFTEEN | Where I am Now 131
SIXTEEN | My New Goals 133

CHAPTER ONE
Dear America

DEAR AMERICA,
    Thank you for the aspirin that you provided when you noticed that I had a headache, it worked. What is your remedy for a scarred soul? Most of my life I have lived with a scarred soul. Outside my window there is a protest. Surprisingly, this time it is global, because another man that looked like me was murdered by a police officer. This time my name is George Floyd.

    I sit within the comfort of my four walls feeling the protesters discomfort. I am proud, yet tired. I have dodged the clutches of police all my life, and I barely made it to live to talk about it. The life of a Black man is a stand-alone protest. Post-Civil War genocide was the end goal of Racist America. The moment descendants of Africans in America no longer worked for free, genocide became the unspoken answer. Each American institution embodied a building block within its construct aimed at stopping Blacks from achieving equality.

    I recognize my significance in uplifting my people. My life gives testament to protest, while my drive testifies of the strength of my people. This is the first in my life I have witnessed people regardless of color stand up in unity for me. I take time to honestly ponder and ask myself if this is what it feels like to be loved and not targeted. We knew, America, that one day it would come. I can only take so much of your pain. My consistent forgiveness is because I love you, but let's be clear: this, my love, is domestic abuse. I will never understand why you refuse to leave me with any dignity. My ancestors gave you all they had, and they endured your pride, yes, your crushing pride, nevertheless you brought us pain. Our love is not mutual.

You have purposely turned your head to the ills of my people, the atrocities you have inflicted, yet, acting as if we created the conditions we live. We know the facts of how we arrived at this condition. True to your stance of an abuser, there lacks consistent change. You redlined our neighborhoods, watered down our education, incarcerated us, and broke up our homes with your discriminatory welfare system. You control the music created by our poets, while brutally policing our neighborhoods. However, what you did not expect was our propensity for greatness.

Today, things are different. We have learned through your trickery: not to ask for anything but to take what we want. We are taking back our families, communities, our talents, our economics, and most important of all, our narratives. For years, we have requested human decency, only to be mocked and plotted against inhumanely. Today it is no longer a request, it is a mandate. We do not fear death. Racism is not part of our motive, it is yours. We want to be treated with respect. It is simple. We understand people are different. We can coexist with others in peace and harmony. We are not savages, but we carry the weight of your oppression which silently says that we are.

We are in a time where you, America, are now forced to pay attention to the mess you have made. Your ears need to be open and your hands ready to work for change. There are three things that fall at your feet of responsibility: 1) help remedy the psychological damage you have done to the people in our communities, 2) assist in the building of our economics, and 3) give us what you owe us!

We are at the bottom fighting for crumbs; survival is our cornerstone. We are descendants of people who were the purest of victims that you have ever victimized. With your aid, the frustration and anger has passed down generation to generation. My peers are blindly caught in a cycle of mistreatment from those who took an oath to protect and serve us. I don't understand their thinking. I can only come to the summation that they are doing what they are told to do. I come from a community that this country has openly condemned. No matter how good our hearts are and how hard some people have tried to conform to the dominant culture way of living, nothing seems to work. Even those that we see that are liked for doing something great are walking a tightrope. It's mentally draining, but I've learned how to balance the mental pressure by deciding to be me and numbing myself to the fact that traps have been set and the good people I know who see it seem to not really know. We are forced to experience the highest level of self-consciousness and still expected to work confidently.

The only ones of us who are able to be themselves seem to be the ones who don't care what you think about them personally, and society has found a way to condemn them for their strength, even used drugs and the prison industry to break them down. It does something to me when I look at the constitution and realize that my people weren't included for a long time. That would be okay if there weren't so many daily reminders.

Please remember that my people and I are working our way through the tangled webs you have weaved with the hopes of keeping us in our place. It's hard not to think that my life would have been completely different had there not been an evil plan conspired against us. Although times have changed, and I live in a very different time than my ancestors, I charge myself with the task of not forgetting that many of them were robbed of their hopes and dreams. So, it is on me to not only succeed by living the American dream but building so that those who come after me don't have to suffer.

Because of this country's marketing and your strategic planning, people of my hue have had to find ways to psychologically adapt and deal with the environment you created for us. Just think, the victims of your system had to endure the most common plight when it comes to building a family while at the same time questioning their existence. I'm compelled to believe that you are astonished at any man who was able to create something beautiful out of these conditions. Personally, thanks to Barack Obama, the Jay-z's, Lebron James, Robert Smiths, and all the black women who speak out on behalf of our people, I know that I am in alignment with my cause. Things are changing in this country and soon.

CHAPTER TWO
Hello

I SIT IN AWE! I received a call from my agent informing me that a few companies are interested in my services. I am a television producer. It is an exciting career that I enjoy. I am not where I want to be professionally, but I am on my way. My agent's call is important to me, and a source of pride. His call marks a career milestone. It signifies that I am making a mark in this industry and my name is gaining recognition.

I received my co-executive producer title at the end of 2018. I began working in this industry as a production assistant in 2013. A year later I received my first associate producer job on BET Sunday Best, afterward I continued my career as one of the producers of the Real Housewives of Atlanta. It took five years to get to where I am today. Some say it was too fast. I say, who can place a timeline on God's design? I have witnessed plenty of people make strides in their own time, or some would say in their due season. Either way, I worked my butt off and I continue to do so!

I am not a stranger to hard work. I became conscious of my need to work hard early in my work history, because I lacked formal education. I did not complete high school, nor did I complete college. Although I received my General Education Diploma (GED), my lack of formal education is one of those things that I can be self-conscious about. In the back of my mind, I sometimes wonder what I missed not attending school. However, my lingering insecurity is the catalyst which makes me a quick learner. I have always found ways to educate myself and apply information to compensate for what I perceived as a shortcoming. I found ways to maneuver until I was able to find out what I needed to know. Thank God for smartphones and the internet. I consider myself a self-educated person and so far, my methods have brought me here, to a place of success. Honestly, my life does not make much sense to me but is, and has been, an interesting journey.

I began my career as a 29-year-old production assistant. I primarily worked in reality shows, but I also worked as a production assistant on a couple of Tyler Perry movies. Between the movies and reality TV, I found my blessing in reality television. My job was to do whatever I was told to do by pretty much anyone on set. I loved it until I realized that I wanted to produce. I started ear hustling, that is slang for eavesdropping on conversations, and going above and beyond my assigned duties to learn all there was to learn regarding being a producer. It paid off, as my career expanded, and I began to move up in the industry.

Anyone who works in production understand the difficulties that are inherent to the work, yet on the hardest days I remain grateful. Many of my colleagues are unaware of the road I have traveled along my career path. I remained private about my journey for two reasons. First, I did not want to be judged, and unable to secure job opportunities. Second, I was mentally fighting with myself. I was in transition from limited possibilities to the sky is the limit. The life I lived before working in television is a testament of how finding strength will help you climb from low places and soar. The person I am and the hunger that I brought to this business was cultivated in the life I had before this. That part of my life is where I ultimately learned that if you continue loving and chipping away at the hard things about life, you will find your miracles.

I never read a book where someone spoke about mental transition. More specifically the mental transition which happens when people are promoted in their profession. There are times throughout my career where I have felt isolated, thus leading me to think my perception of life is unique through my experiences. My perception colored and shaped my reality to see things a certain way. I have always felt that this was unfortunate. I say unfortunate because it has taken me time to uncover, recover, and discover my authenticity. I know I am not alone in this journey of self-awareness. Many Black men and women have been traumatized to a point where they have lost their true selves to simply survive the trials that are part of being Black in America. I too was once there. Although there is a definite race barrier, lack of experience as well as training while trying to gain footing in your career can be a problem. Furthermore, the lack of Black representation and mentors left me feeling as though I was climbing this ladder alone. As time went on, my perspective broadened and expanded as I began to see what life is like; I learned that there is more than one side to every story. This allowed me to understand that transition requires letting go of what is no longer useful and building on what remains. In my industry this requires mental agility and quick thinking.

Moreover, for me specifically, I learned that sometimes you just have to go with your gut, commit to the journey, or face your issues. You are not always going to have the right answer, but you have the spirit to accomplish whatever it is you desire. In my case I felt like once I began on my own, God started guiding me through the process. Although I am not exactly sure of the journey of everyone I grew up with in my neighborhood or at school I witnessed paths that were tragic and hard that my friends often traveled. It was confusing to me as I struggled to ascend from Ground Zero to become something in life. Especially coming out of an environment where I was always told that I was nothing. Furthermore, this narrative was reinforced because I rarely saw successful people who looked like me.

I was born into a home where the support system was fractured. I came home to my mother and my siblings, my father was not in the home. I only had my grandmother as my extended family; therefore, I was left under the supervision of my mother. I was affected by whatever her perception of life was, or whatever her circumstances were. My mom had a lot going on, so she didn't have much time to invest in me at the time I began to gain some understanding of what was happening in our world. She was trying to raise six kids and working to get out of poverty. That was a really demanding life, and I noticed the stress from those demands around four years old.

As a young kid, I assumed the responsibility of helping my family. I remember being six years old helping with my grandmother, who developed full-blown Alzheimer's. She and I spent a lot of time together; and family members would come by to check on us. My daily life consisted of me, her, and my siblings. Sometimes she would get lost and I would have to find her. I remember that it took me a while to understand that she was having episodes. What I mean by episodes is that she would forget who I was for a moment and I would keep talking to her until her memory came back to her. I'm not sure if it really worked or if I got accustomed to trying to reason with her in the time it took for her to snap back. As a young kid, in this situation, I quickly learned to think like an adult as much as possible. My environment required me to be responsible, so to make up for my lack of experience as well as my lack of complete understanding, I keenly observed everything that happened around me.

I knew that at any moment things could change with my grandmother, so it was rare that I would relax and not be on guard. A lot of times, I watched my friends out in the streets playing and carefree, something I could not understand. Even the times that I did go outside I was concerned and wondering if she was okay. I'd closely watch the house distracted from play with my friends.

When I was with her, I was her eyes and ears because I knew what she was dealing with mentally, and I knew that the people we were around did not know. I was afraid of what they would do, so I felt like a protector. I did not want her to be mistreated, physically hurt, or taken advantage of, therefore I ensured her safety as best as could. Instead of my grandmother protecting me and taking care of me, it was role reversal. That made me attentive to how everyone around me treated each other. I wanted to do kid things; I wanted to think like a kid and not have responsibilities, but that was not the reality of my circumstances.

Some of my most profound memories stem from my grandmother having an episode which transported her back to her past. I would know this was happening because she would find me, take me in the room, and barricade the door. She would then sit in a corner with me in her arms and cry, "They are coming!" In the beginning it was scary! I thought someone was coming, but after I realized it was her memories, I learned to console her.

During this time, I remember wondering what it was about me that life put me in the situation I experienced with my grandmother. However, I often felt as though there was something in my spirit telling me that my life would be different. Looking back, I now recognize the special connection with my grandmother. I was supposed to be in that barricaded room with her, the experience gave me insight into her former life that others did not have the honor to know. I was given a chance to become the close protector of someone I knew who loved me.

I had no choice but to try to find solutions to problems I did not understand and was ill-equipped to handle. I didn't run from the situations, instead I dealt with them as God gave me the strength and fortitude needed. I think that is what pushed me in the direction of moving toward success. Although I made mistakes, I forced myself to deal with things I knew nothing about, this gave me the aptitude to be a quick learner, and an agile thinker. Each day potentially presented new problems or situations that were beyond my scope of childlike understanding. Nevertheless, I was learning and sharpening my life skills daily dealing with them. Yeah, they were difficult situations, but I pushed through.

As I reflect, I consider being responsible at a very young age both a gift and a curse. The duty of playing my role in the family taught me how to be attentive to the needs of other people. Being a caretaker isn't easy, but for me, as an adult, it seems to be natural. I closely watched my grandmother. Thinking ahead with anticipation of what was to come regarding her, became my second nature. For instance, I understood she would get up and walk around in the middle of the night, so I started setting out her favorite things, like Sanka coffee and Kit Kat candy bars. I would also check the back door to make sure it was locked properly. As a child, I became a light sleeper.

My responsibilities spilled over to my siblings; I developed the mindset that I had to help my mom with them. I rarely thought about myself regarding what I needed help with. In some ways my reality of responsibility kept me out of trouble. There were situations where I would be with my friends and real trouble was ahead, but I would think about how much I needed to be home to help my mom, so I would talk myself out of doing what I knew would get me into trouble with the law or get me hurt.

As a kid, when my grandmother used to take long walks, her favorite thing to do was to look through trash cans for cans and newspapers. She would often walk very far from home and get lost. It would be my job to help her remember who I was and to convince her to come back home. It wasn't long before I learned how to keep my eyes on my surroundings so we would not get too lost. I can recall days when my grandmother would bring strangers into the house. I would wake up some mornings and she would be cooking breakfast with a stranger lady and some kids that I'd never seen before, and she worried if they were family members. I know that this was from Alzheimer's.

My grandmother was a brown-skinned woman, kind of slim, and I remember she had a very low haircut but used to wear a wig. She was a very careful person, but as time goes on my memories get very vague. Sadly, there are things I remember that override the good things. One time I was at home with my grandmother, just me and her alone. It had to be around like 9 or 10 o'clock at night, and we were on the couch watching television. We heard a knock at the door and when we looked out there was a guy making a lot of noise. I was terrified. My grandmother said, "Who is it? Is it my son Eugene?"

When he heard her say my uncle's name, he started to tell her that he was my Uncle Eugene. My grandmother tried to push me off the door, but I held on. Then he told her to go to the window and she tried to open it, but I pushed her before she could get a grip. Since I wasn't letting her open the front door or the window, she told him to meet her at the back door. I went to the kitchen before my grandma could and jumped on the 2x4 that we had holding the door locked. I remember her hitting me to get me off the door. The guy was at the back door knocking. I yelled that the police were on the way and after a few curse words I didn't hear him anymore. Not long after my grandmother snapped back and acted as if everything was normal. She didn't remember what happened. That was the moment I really noticed how deeply Alzheimer's can affect someone.

Walking through the neighborhood and picking berries was one of my grandmother's favorite pastimes, and it was something we did quite often. I remember one time going to someone's house, but I'm not sure where it was. We were in the middle of their field picking berries, and a lady looked out the window and told us to get off her land. My grandmother was not paying attention, but I was being very nice and respectful to the lady and told her we were going to leave. You can imagine how scared I was, wondering what was going to happen, because I knew these people didn't understand that my grandmother had this mental condition. It wasn't long before the lady's son came out of the house to try to remove us off the property. As he ran over to us, I realized he was an older guy. He was yelling at my grandmother to leave, and I explained to him that she didn't remember anything and asked him just to be nice. It wasn't long before he understood that I was telling the truth. Often, I was amazed at how badly the disease had taken over my grandmother and how oblivious to everything around her she became. She was still able to do the things that she loved and no matter how sick she had gotten, she never ceased being nice to people.

I wasn't with my grandma very long, so there's not much I can say, but I do remember how much of an effect she had on me. As an adult now, I look back and wonder how different my life would have been had she not been sick. After my grandmother I really don't feel that there was anyone else to take care of me until around the age of 15 or 16. It was the beginning of a different life when she moved to my auntie's house in Houston, Texas, and it would be a long time before I would see her or talk to her again.

I can see that my experience with my grandmother honed my people skills and my navigation skills. As a young kid I had to learn how to talk to people that we would encounter in the neighborhood, and I learned that there are many types of people.

Losing the people who were close to me was not only difficult but hurtful. Death was a part of life in my neighborhood. Too often someone I knew passed away or was killed, sometimes it seemed as though this was a daily occurrence. However, it was not every day that someone close to me would die. When someone close to me or special to me died I was overshadowed with sadness for my loss. My special people were those who paid attention to me, who made me feel like I mattered. They didn't have me around for duties; they just had me around because of me, and their love for me.

The first death that was hard for me to handle was the death of my Uncle Gene. When I was a kid he used to come around, and when he would see me, he would smile, hug me, and ask how I was doing. I never doubted that he cared about me. One time I had a fight with my older sister in front of the projects where we lived. I hit her in the back with a 2x4 piece of wood and in return she beat me to my knees, she then went back next door and continued hanging with her friends. It was a funny situation! After recovering, I went into the apartment and called my Uncle Gene. Not long after, he arrived to pick me up and console me. He took me to my favorite restaurant at the time, Rally's, then dropped me at my cousins' house. I have never forgotten that day because he showed up for me. In that situation, in a so-called normal family, a boy would have called his hero, his father. I didn't have a father, but I had Uncle Gene. Unc was my favorite.

I distinctly remember the day I found out he had died. My uncle and aunt had planned to drive from Minnesota to Texas, on to Chicago, and then drop me off in St. Louis. I had visited my dying grandmother in Texas, so I was preparing myself for her departure and had adjusted to seeing her for the first time in a long time. After visiting my grandmother, we stopped at my aunt's house in Chicago. When we arrived at my aunt's house, I was in the car asleep. My cousin Adrienne woke me up and asked me to come sit on the porch with her. While sitting there talking, she suddenly shared with me the bad news that my Uncle Gene had passed away in the hospital.

Shocked and in disbelief, I got up and ran into the house to the phone. I called my uncle's phone number several times. After he didn't answer, I realized that my cousin would not joke about something like that, and he really was gone. Again, I found myself feeling like life was not fair. I was headed to St. Louis to live with my Uncle Gene and was looking forward to it. Now I was really questioning God. I was 14 and tired, drained from having to be responsible, drained from having to prove myself to adults who I thought were supposed to love me, and drained from wanting someone to look at me as important. My Uncle Gene and my grandmother were the two who did it consistently, and now no longer had them by my side, encouraging me.

My grandmother passed not too long after Uncle Gene and I felt alone in the world. I vividly remember the day of my grandmother's wake as well as her funeral. Her funeral was the first I can ever recall attending. I walked into the funeral home and saw my Uncle Dell leaning over my grandmother's casket, crying. I didn't see her lying in the casket until he stood up to wipe his tears. I was immediately freaked out; it was a weird feeling. Taking my time, I slowly made my way to the casket. Seeing her was hard to process. We hear about death and know it is coming, but it is a different type of feeling when it is a special person in your life. I lay on the church bench to cry, as I was lying there, I heard the doors of the church open and I heard chains. I remember wondering why I heard, of all things, chains, in a church, at a funeral, more specifically my grandmother's funeral. When I looked up, I saw my older brother Jamour dressed in an orange jumpsuit, handcuffed, with two cops standing next to him. That was an immediate sensory overload for me. I had not seen him in a while, but this was unlike anything I had ever seen. He asked the cops if he could hug me. At that point I became confused about my own tears; I was crying for the two of them. Looking back, I realize I was standing in between two different types of deaths.

•

CHAPTER THREE
Welcome to My Broken Home

IF YOU DON'T understand everything going on in your environment, eventually you will. As you gain understanding, it will alter your belief system in some way regardless of how old you are! You will either have a stronger belief in what you already thought, or you will come to an awakening that will create either a sense of fear or a sense of confidence. In my case, I went through both emotions before finding a solution.

My childhood differed from that of a typical child. These differences were marked by specific occasions that I remember experiencing at a young age. Not only did I become my grandmother's primary caretaker, I did not attend preschool or kindergarten like other children my age at the time. When I attended school, I went straight to first grade. Additionally, around the age of five, I started noticing that there were some missing pieces to my family. The kids at school and my friend next door had a father and grandparents. I only had my mother and grandmother. Around the age of eight, my older brother went to prison, and not long after that, my older sister ran away.

My mother, at the time, had five children. I am the third child. I taught and protected myself, my grandmother, and my younger siblings.

When we lived in the Peabody projects, it was the first time I remember living in a home with my immediate family. My grandmother had been sent to live in Texas with my aunt, so I no longer had to worry every day if she was okay. It was time for me to go to first grade. School was a completely new experience for me. First, I was in a class with White kids and had White teachers, something I had to adjust to because I was not around White people much. Secondly, I did not have much experience being away from family hours at a time. I made a fairly quick adjustment; I wasn't a shy kid. I was actually talkative, and I have a reputation for that today. I remember being amazed to be in a class with other kids to talk to, and play with at recess. I can still picture my first-grade classroom. One day while at field day, I got into a fight with another kid, and the school yard attendant wasn't happy at all. He was so angry that he told the principal, an old, tall, blond, White guy. I don't remember his name, but I do remember them taking me out of recess into a room that I think was the janitor's office. The principal told me that I could not go back out until recess ended. He asked me if my mother and father approved of my behavior. While he was talking, I was crying because I was terrified of being in that room and he was a stranger to me. After field day was over, school was out, it was time to go home. I got my things and headed for the bus. While en route I saw the White kid, I had a fight with walking with his parents, and that made me think about what the principal asked me. On my bus ride home, I realized that I really didn't have a dad. The thought was new to me. I did not know how to feel about an old fact my six-year-old mind newly realized.

My bus stop used to drop us off in front of Clinton Junior High School behind the projects. Often, we would pull up to witness a major fight happening. It was not uncommon to see one of the kids' parents standing by refereeing the battle. My older brother and sister went to the school, so one of them would be there waiting on me. Often it was my sister. Although she was there, the walk home was scary. We had to pass junkies, dope dealers, and older dudes who tried to holler at my sister. This time getting off the bus was different for me. I now walked home thinking about how scary school was today. It appears that day my eyes opened to the reality of my environment. I walked with my sister noticing multiple dangers in the neighborhood where we lived. We walked, and I was painfully aware of the reasons I should have a dad at the bus stop waiting on me every day.

I did not say anything to my mom; for one thing, she was busy working and fighting with my older siblings, specifically my older brother. He was hanging in the projects, and she wanted him to stay in the house. As a first grader I got the notion that I was going to have to take care of myself. For a while I started paying attention to all the older guys I would see. I assumed they all were dads, and I assumed they were all in their kids' lives, and that made me question what was wrong with me.

As I observed the family dynamics around me, I realized that all the kids on my street had some type of father figure in their lives. My friend who lived in the apartment to the left of us had a father who lived with him. Even though I hated hearing his parents argue through the wall, I envied the times I would see my friend come outside dressed in his baseball uniform with his dad behind him carrying his equipment and snack. The friends to the right--there were about six of them--were Black and Native American and all of them were named after the Jackson 5. Their father didn't live with them, but he would stop by on occasion to bring them food and money. My older brother and sister had a different dad than me and my younger siblings. I don't have any memory of their father before we moved to the projects, but he started coming around. One day I got the courage to ask my mom why I did not have a father, and she had no answer. At the time I was not aware my younger sister, who was two years under me, had the same father.

I could tell that it bothered my mom when I asked her. I started hearing her whispering and arguing with someone. I assumed it was that dude (the guy she said was my dad), or it was my brother and sister's father. My older siblings' father came by to visit one day, and she pulled him away from me. When they came back, he had a distressed look on his face and suddenly invited me to go fishing with him. He took me with him a few times. It was cool, but we did not have major bonding moments. One time he left me with his mother and sisters, who were nice. The last time we hung out, which was the last time we hung-out, I remember sitting in the car and waiting while he went into the alley to talk to a few of his friends. That was the only attempt I remember my mother making to have a man try and connect with me.

I had constant reminders that I was part of a broken family. One day my friend next door invited me to go to baseball tryouts with him, and my mom let me go. After tryouts, we went to one of his family members' houses. There I found out that the coach was his uncle, and at the table in the dining room were his grandparents, four of them. His mother's and father's parents. I believe this was my second time seeing someone with both parents and two whole sets of grandparents. The whole evening, I did not want to play with the kids, I stayed around the old folks. I'm sure they thought it was weird. I spoke of my grandmother, hoping they would understand. Things were not the same for me after that. I wanted everything my friend had. When my mom would discipline me, I would be sadder than normal because I was now feeling bad for myself, sorrowful that there was no one to come wipe my tears after a whooping. I was overly emotional when it came to certain things and I didn't know why. I was always in my head and wanting someone to give me undivided attention. Looking back, I think that was a symptom of growing up in an uncertain environment and having a limited support system that could nurture me. Things were not always stable around me. Living in the projects contributed to my chronic feelings of instability. The energy alone is something you never forget. Around this time my mom was pregnant with my baby brother, and this is when things changed. My older brother got locked up and was sent to prison. My mom was hurt. She decided to move us to a house on the opposite side of town. Not long after we moved into the new place, my older sister moved out on her own. That left me, my mom, and my two younger siblings. My mom became stricter on me. I don't think she noticed how open my eyes were becoming to our environment. I understood things beyond my years by dealing with my grandmother, so as things changed in the house, I felt it. Honestly, I was uncomfortable not having anyone to protect me. Going to school every day was already dangerous; even the old heads sitting by the dumpster used to tell me to run to my bus stop and to run home. One time I got in a fight with an older kid and his mom stood by and told him to hit me in the mouth, and he followed orders. I walked home crying with a bloody lip, again pitying myself. At that time, I had gone through the process of my reality, realizing that I did not have a whole family and as a finale, I had watched it fall apart. I wanted my family to be together, but little did I know I was at the threshold of my journey facing life's harsh realities. Although I know my situation was not unique to me, as a child I felt like I was going through it alone and nobody understood.

    My viewpoint of the world was very narrow. It got to a point where it seemed like there was not an ounce of positivity around me. I stopped believing that God existed because I did not feel like he heard any of my mom's prayers. We had so little that I would pray for simple stuff, like someone giving my mom five dollars for gas, five dollars was hard to come by some days.

The weird thing about me is I can't really tell if I was affected by not having a father. It's not something I frequently thought about. What bothers me the most, is the things I went through with my mother, the things about me that she never was able to pay attention to, the life struggles we experienced together, stuff like that. I do remember resenting her because I wanted her to support me the way I wanted her to show support, however, she chose to show support the way she felt she should show support. Looking back, that was a true lesson in love and relationships. I learned to lean on her words, not her actions.

Today I have so much respect for a single woman with multiple kids. It is a challenging job, and no one should ever have to do it alone. My point of view at that time was one of a child and I had little information or understanding of what it was like being an adult. My interpretation of the decision the adults around me made derived from how I felt. I remember certain things because of how it made me feel. Being the third of six children, I did not get much quality time with my mother. By age six my days of being my mother's helper had begun. At a young age I felt like my mom really needed me to step up and think about others. That wasn't a bad thing, although I do recall one time asking myself who was I important to? I was an intuitive kid; I think that helped me be a good caregiver because I was in touch with my surroundings. I had the ability to often anticipate the needs of others, coupled with the desire to help those in need.

CHAPTER FOUR
Trying to Understand

IN THIS CHAPTER and throughout this book I will talk at length about my mother. I want to be clear that I am writing my truth and there are moments I found very hard to understand the way I was parented. Nevertheless, I love my mother wholeheartedly! She and I went through a rough time in life together and we both made it through in our own way. What you are about to read is from my point of view of the things that happened in my life. I hope that if you have any issue with your parents or grandparents, I pray that you address them, forgive them, and move forward. Life isn't easy for anyone. Empathy and understanding will give you a peace of mind, as well as forgiveness.

The older I get the more I realize what it's like to have to make decisions for yourself and other people. As a child I was completely unaware of the real challenges a person faces being a parent, and now I have a deep respect for anyone who dedicates themselves to being the best parent possible.

My mom is smart. She has a strong personality that she took with her when she enlisted into the military. She gained a wealth of knowledge while serving in the military. I can only imagine her internal battle with being a single mother of six children and living in some environments that many would consider dangerous. As a small kid, she was a fun parent. Although she didn't have much to give, she could make a grocery store trip seem like an excursion. She would always give me jewels to live by, which came daily and randomly. Often, she was inspired by whatever situation she was dealing with. I know it was difficult being both mom and dad, but she put her all into it when she was in our presence. One thing I learned from my mom was that I should never accept being in unhappy conditions; life has more to offer. When we'd fall on hard times, she made it a point for me to recognize how bad things were, then tell me that this wasn't the way it's supposed to be. I couldn't understand how or why things were that way for us. It was frustrating because in a sense I was forced to look at the negative things in life, but I didn't have context as to what led us there. I learned how to worry when things got bad. Each experience presented different obstacles that seemed unavoidable. I got to a point where I felt it was normal for the lights and water to be cut off. Each time those things happened I could see the hurt in my mother's eyes. She didn't like asking people for help but was forced too. After she received help from people, she'd become very quiet.

Her favorite thing to do was to drive when she needed to think. She would have us all get dressed and we would get in the car and ride around the city, especially in good neighborhoods. My favorite days were when she would drive us through rich people's neighborhoods and point out the best houses. To this day I'm a sucker for a beautiful neighborhood. They are what symbolize success to me. No matter what I accomplish in life, I won't feel as if I made it until I'm in a house with at least five bedrooms, green perfectly manicured grass and a 2-car garage. Growing up having a stable home that the whole family could live in was something I wished for often. To this day those car rides are vivid memories that never get old.

My mom taught me how to dream and appreciate beauty. However, she was very aware of our current environment and made it her business to reinforce respect. Today I'm thankful my mom never hesitated to discipline any of us. I hated getting whoopings so much I started grabbing the belt. She became stricter after my older brother went to prison. I was rarely allowed out of her sight unless she had something to do, and when she left, I was to babysit. I was too afraid of her to do anything that I knew she wouldn't like, so she didn't have to worry. If I had a friend she didn't like, then it was no question if I could hang with them or not. She let me and them know that it wasn't allowed. I don't think my mom was afraid of much.

As a little kid I noticed a lot but was accepting and happy whenever my mom was around. But the older I got I started seeing other characteristics in her that helped me understand why things were the way they were. When you look at a person's life, their circumstances are either a good indicator of how they make decisions, or their circumstances dictate their decision-making.

My relationship with my mother was one that I've been thinking about and trying to understand for a very long time. As far as I can remember, as a kid I was a helping hand. I don't know much about my siblings' life before she had me. When I did think about it, I assumed it was better for them, and by the time I was old enough to be a part of what was going on my mother wasn't working much. She looked for work, but at the same time, she would spend time with my father or the guy who was supposed to be my father. I don't know much about him, he's never done anything that I know of that has helped us, but I know that he was around.

Only around my birthday and holidays did I question if I was going to receive anything from him, which never happened. I didn't feel too bad about it because I was accustomed to not celebrating my birthday anyway. It wasn't until I was nine years old when I had my first birthday party. My mom's friend came over and found out it was my birthday. He told us to get dressed and meet him at Chuck E Cheese. When we got there, he had what seemed like his whole family waiting. It was amazing a bunch of nice strangers celebrating my birthday with me. A few days later my mom's friends stopped by the house and saw me outside. He asked me if I received anything from my father. I told him I didn't know the guy. He reached in his pocket and gifted me a hundred-dollar bill. Until this day I kinda think that was out of sympathy.

See, I never told my mom how I truly felt about not having a father. The main reason was because as far as I can remember there was always some confrontation between the two, and although I don't remember who told me, I was well aware that he denied that I was his child. After hearing that and seeing that they still had some type of situationship, I didn't trust that she wouldn't tell him what I had to say. The situation was confusing. She told me that I needed to just speak to him, and once I agreed she put me on the phone, but he would hear my voice and hang up. Then later he would have someone else call the house and ask for her.

That went on for years. I'd hear them fight on the phone often but see him pull up outside the house to pick her up. The older I got the more I questioned the situation. It became hard to understand how it was that he could reject me so blatantly and then still come around when he wanted. It got to the point where whenever the phone rang, and I saw his number on the caller Id I would mute the phone. I knew that if he got hold of my mother that day, she would leave or the atmosphere in the house would change. It got so crazy that she took us to get a blood test just to prove to him she was right, but that didn't change anything. I eventually realized that my mother had a deep love for this guy, and she hoped that he would eventually accept us. Honestly that whole ordeal made me feel miserable about myself. Having to hear some guys say that I wasn't his child and making threats to keep me away from him was a heck of thing to try to comprehend. For a while I thought my mom was in the wrong and just pushing us off on this guy. He was so adamant about not wanting to have anything to do with us. I knew there was no way he was lying.

One day I found out partly why he denied me. I was a child that he had outside of his marriage, and I had a sister the same age as me. Years would go by and through my younger sister I'd meet more of his children. By then I didn't feel any connection to anyone other than my siblings I grew up with and three of the many I met along the way. I went to my sister's graduation, the one who was my age, and there was an older guy there who she said was our brother. I had my younger brother with me who reached to shake his hand and the guy pulled back. He wasn't happy. That sealed the deal for me. Whoever I hadn't already met on that side I will never know. Had it not been for my mother and my younger sister I would have never made any attempts at all.

The biggest issue I had growing up was seeing the effect that my father had on my mother. If he'd call, she would make herself available. I honestly believe she did that hoping that one day he would accept me and my siblings. Ultimately it would be a failed mission on her end. For a long time, I was very angry with her over that. It took me until the age of 19 to address her and have a full conversation. I didn't walk away with any understanding, but it felt good knowing that I'd told her how I felt. I didn't like having those feelings toward her. After my grandma died, she was my only parent.

Education was not a priority. I went to school to socialize. When I attended school, I was a good student to some teachers and a demon to others. My mom didn't have much money, so I did not have anything special. My clothes caused me so many problems that I lost interest in being in school. My classmates constantly made fun of whatever I wore. On the other hand, my teachers noticed when I applied myself. They noticed the high scores I received on my exams, so when I did not do well, they became concerned. What I never told them was that the many fights I had in school all started in class. Although I became known in every school I attended, I had to fight to get my respect, so I spent a lot of class time plotting how I was going to win the fight. In 7th grade I was attending Northwest Junior High School. All my teachers referred me for the Scared Straight program, although I wasn't doing anything criminal, just fighting. One day my group took a visit to the county jail. They took us all the way into the jail, through the processing and on the block with the prisoners. That experience did not make me afraid, I did however, see that guys who were locked in there had become way too comfortable. I knew jail was not for me, but it did not stop the fights. That led me to getting suspended so much that my mom got tired of taking me back to school. Looking back, I don't think I ever mentally bought into the idea of being a student. Yes, I was at school, following my schedule and doing what I was told to do but my mind was not there. I gained a love/hate relationship with all schooling. In my life I was put out of three school systems: St. Louis, Memphis, and Minneapolis. I was bumped to 11th grade when I went to LA, but I eventually quit for the last time. I had a meeting with the superintendent in St. Louis and he decided to put me out because I looked him directly in his eyes while he was talking to me. He got offended and asked why I did that. I didn't respond, which made things worse. In my head I wanted to tell him that my mom told me to always look a man in his eyes when talking, but I didn't want to make her look bad, so I said nothing.

    She was furious with me, and when we got in the car, she lost it. I never told my mom that I had given up on school long ago; it was too much. It was hard focusing on classwork when I was mostly thinking about what life was like outside of school. I didn't get haircuts all the time, which was another source of embarrassment, but

I still had to go to school, so some days I would skip and go over to a friend's house who lived close by to hang out until school was out then go home. I'd make it home in time to catch the call from the school, so my mom didn't know for a while.

I was 11 years old when I first started drinking and smoking. At the time, I spent more time hanging out with my older cousins, who were more like my brothers. They had to share everything with me. My clothes were their hand-me-downs, which was good because they wore the latest styles, and I did not have trouble with people making fun of my appearance as I once had while in school. Their mom was my mom's cousin. When I was at their house, those were the days I had the most fun. We played family games, took zoo trips, had ice cream from McDonald's and anything she could think of to keep us active. Soon that all would change. As we grew older, our neighborhood was taken over by police and heroin. It would not be long before a lot of the guys, I grew up with were dead. When my older cousin Gaylon was murdered at 16, everything changed. His mom became another person. When he died, I felt like I had lost a brother. Something deep in me changed, and I saw life differently.

Gaylon was someone, I thought, could do no wrong. We were close in age, two years apart, and our birthdays were two days apart. Everything he did I wanted to do. Heroin roared through our neighborhood like an angry lion. It consumed and emptied the soul of all it touched. While this was happening, Gaylon started hanging out with a different crowd, and suddenly I could no longer tag along. I then started to hang more with his older brother, whose focus was on chasing girls. My mom did not like that we would hang out in areas that were gang infested. It was an unfortunate truth that most of those areas were in the Black communities in St. Louis. A string of murders happened and there were only a few guys left alive on our street. For me that's when things got real, and I knew that something had to change. I never thought only about myself. I wanted things for me and my folks to be better.

Being self-conscious was a hard task for me because I experienced a dichotomy when thinking about it. One side of me cared what people thought. The other side of me caught on early in life that if I didn't have my own back I would always be in danger, so fuck what people thought. Eventually I leaned toward having my own back and not caring what others thought of me, however, people began to say I was arrogant. I thought that was both good and bad; it depended on who said it. I never thought I was arrogant. I felt like I was trained and justified to be the way I am. When someone has been neglected or mistreated, they will either break down or do the opposite: become stronger. I became stronger. This approach is how I protected myself in the environment I lived. I wanted to be better and stronger for myself. Other people have played a role in my getting to that point by just treating me however they saw fit--and I responded how I saw fit.

What baffles me is that as a kid I was often told to listen and do what I was told. I was taught to look for guidance from others and be quiet. As I got older, I was told not to brag or toot my own horn. I then learned that there are limited people to receive guidance from. As you get older, if you make a mistake, they tear you down. So, I decided that no matter what, I'll do everything I can to keep my strength and not let the world tear me down, even if it is at the expense of being called arrogant. I am wise enough to know that my dealing with others and my reputation go hand in hand, so I know that my arrogance cannot trump my ability to respect and uplift others. I make it my business to treat people well. I also make it my business to be respected. Today, I am 37 years old and I feel like I've lived a lot of life. There are many levels and lessons I have yet to reach; I know I cannot get there alone.

I do not make friends just to get ahead in life. I can honestly say that 90 percent of my friendships are genuine. When I am in awkward places or dealing with someone who I can't be myself with, then things get weird during that moment, and I want to avoid that person or situation. Part of my integrity is to be authentic, because of this I tend to make easy connections to other people.

Being born into a broken home is survivable. It is your life, and you don't know what you are missing. But after a while, when you realize that you are, in fact, missing something, it is a different world. As I started getting older and trying to figure out how to be a man, I started seeing how much my mother didn't understand. My mother really couldn't identify with us, so I feel like her easiest thing was to give me tasks to make me responsible for my brothers and sisters so I wouldn't feel like I was never really paid attention to. In school I fought a lot, and that was because when I was at home, I didn't have much of a social life other than taking care of my brothers and sisters. In school I was preoccupied with making friends rather than being concerned with my work. I had a few teachers who paid attention and made me feel as if I could accomplish something, but other than that, it was nothing but obstacles.

Things I learned in school or the stuff about us as Black people on the news reinforced the difficulty by constantly painting a picture of the struggling Black person in America. I was part of a people America seems to hate.

I learn about slavery and the great accomplishments of my people, but I also learned that they were forced to by somebody else and then the greatness was never really realized. It's even worse that we get one month out of the year to really celebrate our people. When you're in an environment where everything is questionable, your level of confidence is always in jeopardy if you don't get a real understanding of where and who you are.

CHAPTER FIVE
LIMITED GUIDANCE

BEING NEGLECTED TAUGHT me how to love. I love deeply. I remember being told that people often overcompensate when it comes to certain things, they lacked in their life. I think it is true. Until recently I never saw myself as a person who overcompensated for anything. One day a co-worker asked me if I had grown up in a two-parent home. I told him no and asked why. He said that after listening to me talk on the phone to my daughter and other family members he could tell that I communicate in a way where I want the person I am talking with to know I love them. I thought about that for a moment and he was right. It is my principle to try and connect with people. I sometimes go out of my way to show that I care, be it with a stranger or a familiar person. I know what it is like to be in a bad mental space and be around people who see you and treat you like things are normal, when they are not and furthermore, things are chaotic causing unseen pain. I spent so many days in a crazy head space. I automatically consider that people I meet along the way may be going through something challenging.

My mother was a very strong woman who used her words strongly when she needed to. If you did not obey, you would likely get your ass whipped. As a kid I recall her disciplining me the most when I was in school. It was hard to explain to her that my behavior issues stemmed from a couple of things: one, we were poor, so I never really went to school with anything new on and when you go to any city school that can cause problems. Although my teachers told me I was smart, I was distracted. I recall many times the teacher would write on the board, with her back turned, while two or three kids throwing spitballs at me or making jokes and whispering about me. That was hard for me to avoid. Often, I was angry. There always seemed to be people against me, and I was always alone for the most part. It was pretty much the same when I was at home in my neighborhood. When I was at home, my mother paid only so much attention to me, her focus at the time was trying to ensure a roof over our heads and food in our belly. I have two younger sisters and a younger brother, and when they came into my life, I had to be the responsible big brother who was charged with helping take care of them. At one point I found myself looking around to see if anyone would ask me if there was something in life I wanted to do. I started going to school hoping that a teacher would take me under their wing. As a young kid I understood that my mother could not give me the attention that I thought I needed because she had multiple children, so I had to figure out how to keep up my own confidence. She tried tirelessly to make things work. I remember her many times calling people asking for help.

One day I watched my mom as she prayed. At the time, all our utilities were cut off. We had a notice on the door that we had to move out, and there was no food in the house. I was lying on the couch in extreme pain. My stomach was turning into knots. When she finished praying, she went next door to the neighbor's house to get food. This made me wonder what was the purpose of my mom praying, when she seemingly resorted to asking our neighbors for help. It was hard to believe in God when everything bad was happening to us. She prayed hard, but things got worse. Honestly, to this day I still wonder how I kept my faith. My perception of God was skewed watching all the things she had to deal with. She was a strong, prideful person. I am not sure why our lives did not improve, but I know she always talked about God, yet the results that we expected never happened.

As a boy all I had was a mother and her perspective, a woman's perspective. That type of teaching puts a child at a disadvantage. My mother often gave great advice. The advice typically came after an encounter with the man she said was my father. She would give words of wisdom about manhood, pointing out how my father should not behave or act as a man. As I matured, her advice, while profound, fell on deaf ears because I saw her continue to interact with the person who seemingly caused her much pain and anger. I would often question her choices. I found myself silently asking why she chose to hang around my dad.

In my experience, young Black boys who grow up with just their moms are taught to be survivors. Many of the moms are victims of bad parenting, bad relationships, or traumatic situations which have left them with low self-esteem. Often these women raise kids on their own. I believe I was raised by someone who had a few of these experiences, and it affected how she dealt with us. That has made me conscious of how I treat women in my life. My protective senses kick in when around both women and children. I remember how I felt watching my mother and my younger siblings struggle with surviving day to day life.

Since I've been a parent, I realize how it's possible to be a parent and still be in the process of trying to understand yourself.

CHAPTER SIX
Evicted

"**IF YOU'VE EVER** been put out of your home before, then I hope that God blessed you somehow after that. There is nothing like being put out of your house. Having to watch some other people walking into your home and digging through your things is surreal. It feels even more disrespectful when the people throwing your things out have no regard for you as a person. They say to you, "I'm just doing my job!" Now that I'm older I understand that guy. Some of us have no choice but to just do our job, even if it's putting a mother and her children on the streets. If you do not do your job, it can potentially be you being put out of your home. I say this because I understand now, even though I did not understand then. I had a real issue with the guys who came in and threw our things out. I'm over it now, but it was definitely something I'll never forget. I was a young half-asleep boy caught off guard that day."

—MARKUS

We got evicted early one morning while my siblings were at school. It was an unforgettable experience. After seeing how my mother cried about it, the guy she called my dad showed up but didn't get out of the car, the sheriff was throwing our things on the lawn. I realized that day that somehow, some way, I needed to find a way to be able to take care of myself. It wasn't as embarrassing to me that our shit was out in the yard. I was more embarrassed that some dude stuck his head in the bathroom window while I was pissing. I heard of people getting evicted, and I had even seen people's stuff on the curb while riding down the street, but I never tried to imagine what those people went through. Now I knew firsthand. It is quite a simple process. The sheriff breaks in with some needy heartless guys and they just start grabbing stuff. Luckily for me, all my friends were at school that day. The neighbors across the street looked out the window but didn't come out. They looked out for us normally, so I think they didn't come to help because no one knew what to say to my mom, plus most of them were old folks.

Right after we were evicted from the house, I remember my mom pulling on the side of the road and just sitting there. I could tell she was trying to think. We both were stunned at what had just happened. Although I didn't ask her about it, I kept wondering if she had any idea that this was going to happen. I guess she knew what I was thinking, and she started telling me on her own. While she was doing her two-year army tour in Germany, we had family members living in our house. Apparently when she came back, the mortgage was far behind and she never got caught up. I had many more questions to ask but decided not to. After sitting for a while, she pulled off and we checked into a Days Inn motel. We would eventually begin sleeping between that Days Inn and in our car. When we slept in the car, we would park in Wal-Mart parking lots or at the hospital. This is where I learned that a person could stay up for 24 hours and still live because I did it. Things were hazy for a moment. I couldn't understand how God let this happen to us. All my life my mom would do anything she could to help other people. When we would get our stamps, she would have us make sandwiches to take to the homeless people. Now we were the people who needed the sandwiches. To try and keep our heads up, my mom would drive us through really rich neighborhoods so we could see the houses. She would talk to me since I was oldest. She'd tell me that no matter what happened to me I had to remember that I am a man, and a man will always find a way to fix things. I could see her heartbreak in her eyes.

One time I will never forget. We were driving around, nowhere to go, and I was in the back seat looking at her through the rearview mirrors. Before she looked and noticed me watching, I saw a stream of tears start to flow. I told her that everything was going to be okay, but really, I didn't believe it. I took this as a sign that my family was cursed. One night we tried to check back into the Days Inn we would normally go to, and the clerk told my mom he couldn't because the last check didn't clear. She ended up using the money she had for this night to pay the past due. They let us in anyway and even gave us connecting rooms.

That was the beginning of me being self-conscious and embarrassed. It became an everyday thing for me. When my mom didn't want to pull up to the grocery store in an old car full of kids and clothes, then go into the store and spend food stamps, guess who did? Me. I completely understood my mother. I thought about how she must have felt, and I was willing to do anything to try and preserve what dignity she had left. I did not have a choice. I hated getting out of the car for any reason. Pumping gas and going under the hood to open the carburetor valve to get the car started was something I had to do constantly. I wanted to put up a fight, so I didn't have to do it, but I knew that I was all the help she had.

For a while I stopped caring about what I looked like. I got real with myself. We were in real trouble and I was concerned about the thoughts of strangers. How crazy is that? I had to redirect my thinking. The people I was worried about probably wouldn't have noticed me regardless of my circumstances. The only thing I had a right to be concerned about was trying to explain to my friends why we'd gotten kicked out. I came up with a plan for that. I was going to ignore the conversation until they asked. If they pushed to know, I was going to just say my mom didn't tell me why. Little did I know, it would be a while before I would see my friends again. We moved around so much, I had to learn to keep in touch with my friends. Always being in the presence of new people can get a bit depressing because who do you go hang with that you won't have to continually explain yourself or your circumstances?

CHAPTER SEVEN
Memphis

"MEMPHIS HAS A special place in my heart. The days I spent there will forever be with me. I had an encounter with happiness unlike anything I had before. It was a place where I had to prove myself and once I did it, I was highly respected by my peers. My life was one thing at home and another in the streets, and I can honestly say I never had to fake being me."

—MARKUS

My mom got a letter in the mail from the state telling her that someone had reported her, and she had to bring us to them. She tried to hide it from me, but I heard her tell one of her friends how she had to bring us to meet with them. One day we got on the highway and drove down to Memphis. She didn't have a lot of money in her pocket, so she stopped on the way to make a call to see if somebody could Western Union her some money. We continued our trip and made it close enough to get to downtown Memphis near Adams and Manassas. The first place we went was to a woman's shelter. The people at the shelter said they would not be able to take her in because I was with her and normally, they wouldn't take boys, but they would make an exception for my little brother. There was an older guy working at the shelter who told my mother that if she wanted to stay the night that he would keep me at his place. I heard that and immediately looked at her. We both had a bad feeling about him, and she decided that she would find another option. We all got back in the car and headed back down to the Housing Authority. We got there and it was too late in the evening, so the people asked us to come back the next day. My mom was still waiting on some money to feed us and try to get a hotel room, so we hung out nearby. I remember she dug in her purse and found a couple dollars, so she was able to get us some juice and chips on this day. I got out and went to play basketball at the nearby court. Everyone else took a walk, then sat in the car. My mom decided that we were going to stay downtown for the night, so we slept in the car outside of the Housing Authority. Normally when we were sleeping in the car, I would stay awake and keep an eye on everybody, but because I had played basketball, I was exhausted, and I fell asleep. I woke up to hear knocking on the windows and seeing flashlights. I recognized it was the police. My mom let her window down and while she was talking, the other cops reached in and snatched me out of the backseat of the car. My mother started yelling, "He's 13, he's 13!" at the same time the cop was pulling his gun.

After hearing I was 13 years old, the other cop stopped his partner from grabbing me, and they picked me up off the ground. They frisked me down and asked my mother what we were doing. She explained to them that we were waiting to go to the Housing Authority and that we were from out of town. While we were talking to the cops, the security guard from the old folks' building behind us came out and let the cops know that he had been watching over us the whole night and that everything was okay. After the cops left, the security guard invited us to come sit in the lobby for the remainder of the night.

The next day we went down to the Housing Authority and my mom spoke with them. She did not say much when she came back out, but she was not happy. At the time, she had received a Western Union from Chicago. We checked into a nearby hotel, and she made a phone call to my cousins who lived in the city. We had eaten, and at this time I was being a brat, so I started an argument with her. I was mad that she made me come down to Memphis when I could have stayed with my cousins in St. Louis. I did not want to say much, but I felt like this situation with the shelter was going to make things a lot harder for them than it should have been. Then I decided to go ahead and unleash everything on her at that moment. I complained about not being in school, constantly having to move around, and how I felt it was disrespectful that the guy she said was my father was still coming around. I cursed and ran out of the room into the parking lot and walked around the streets.

I felt bad. I knew that things were just as bad for her as us, and she wanted things to be better. I was not sure what had led us here, and I knew that what I had done was not ok. When I returned to the room, she told me that she had spoken with a cousin of ours who invited us to come live with him. My mom's cousin, Moses, lived with his wife, 3 kids and his wife's nephew. When we got to the house, Moses had everything waiting on us with blankets and pillows and we slept on the living room floor. I found out that when he heard that the shelter would not let Mom stay there with me, he told my mom to come stay with them.

Living with Moses was fun. There were a lot of kids in the house and for the most part we all hung out together. In the neighborhood I made a lot of friends. We stayed with Moses for about two months until my mom found a one-bedroom shack about five minutes away from his house.

When she first told me about it, she was happy that it was still in the neighborhood where all my friends lived, and I knew the area very well. There was a certain peace I had living in Double Tree. For the most part, I got along with all the kids I met. They were my real introduction to country Black folks. Although they had a lot of similarities to my friends in St. Louis, they seemed to be more grounded than I was accustomed to, and since my cousin lived on a cove, we all would stay out late some nights and hang on someone's porch. It felt safer and more peaceful than I had felt in a long time. Double Tree has a bad reputation, but to me, it was a safe haven.

My mother, my three siblings, and I all moved into the one-bedroom shack on a piece of land in front of an old lady's house. It was the first time we lived in a house like this. It was about a half an acre of land with a chestnut tree on one side and a persimmon tree on the left, and the driveway was at least a block long. This was country-style living. I was happy because it was the first time in a long time since we had our own place to live. We lived in our car and sometimes in a motel room for about two, maybe three years prior. Although we were all packed in this house, it was ours. The bad thing was, the bathroom and the kitchen were so close, and there was a nest of rats residing comfortably below us. Nevertheless, my mother and sisters took the bedroom. My brother and I slept on the couches in the living room.

Next door, to the house, was a church that we eventually joined, and my mom found a job at FedEx. She enrolled me at Westwood High School. Although we lived in that small house, I believe all of us were happy, finally, not moving around. It was a nice city, and we had a lot of friends. All of us were going to school, Mom was working, and everything was good, for the most part. On the other hand, when I was in school, I had some trouble. I told some guys at school about the neighborhood that I was a part of in St. Louis, and they wanted to fight because they thought I was lying. Eventually they found out that I wasn't lying, and I became pretty popular at school. We went to church three or four times a week and became close to the people there. This was the first time I felt like we were part of a church. I had never experienced this before. The church people were nice and cared about our family. I remember one birthday I was asleep and there was a knock on the door. It was two guys from church. They woke me up because it was my birthday and took me out to buy a pair of shoes. This was the first time I recall someone remembering my birthday and surprising me. I was 13 years old.

When we started attending church in Memphis, it was a positive experience. There were a few families in the church, and everyone was close. Although we attended church several days a week, it wasn't bad, it was more like going to hang with family. I was not as concerned about my clothes. I normally hated going anywhere because of what I had to wear. I was even singing in the choir. This was the first time we, as a family, experienced anything like this. This was a memorable moment in my life. We moved off the streets, where things were chaotic. However, not long after we settled into our yellow house, I found myself extremely happy. It's like I felt the presence of God. We had very little, close to nothing at all, but I was happy. Life felt normal. We lived in a community with a lot of kids, and I knew everyone in the community. I had friends to hang out with, and we went to church every week as a family. Also, I think a big part of it was my mother was in a better headspace than she had been in a long time. I made the basketball team but really couldn't play because the shoes I had were slippery. I did not play sports my mom could not afford. Additionally, my days of babysitting were not over, thus limiting any time I may have had for extracurricular activities. She went to work at night, and I watched my sisters and brother.

Memphis was different from St. Louis. This was the first time I had been confronted with a wake-up call because my skin was a little lighter than others, so I had to prove myself. I had a few fights and by the end of those fights, everyone who was known in school knew me. I ran with a connected crew of dudes. My mom didn't know, but I think she had an inkling.

Ultimately, I would get into a situation at school that would cause me to be suspended indefinitely. The security guard tried to catch me several times skipping. Neither time was he able to catch me, but he did not like me because I would fight at school and I got away with it. One day he saw me hugging a girl and he said that I was grabbing her butt cheeks. He took me to the principal's office, and that was the last straw for him. He was fed up with me, so they sent me home and told me they would let me know when they were ready to bring me back to school. I was suspended indefinitely.

After we had been in Memphis for about a year, my mom was ready to visit St. Louis. We went to see our family and stopped at my aunt's house. While there I called my cousin Gaylon, I hadn't seen him in a while. When I left for Memphis, my aunt, Gaylon, and the rest of their family, had moved to Texas. When we visited, they had moved back to St. Louis. The day I found out they were back in St. Louis, I called them several times. I wanted to see my family and hang out with Gaylon. I was 14 at the time. I asked my mom to take me. Normally she would because she knew how close we were, but for some reason she decided not to take me. I tried to walk out of the house, but she grabbed me and locked me in my aunt's basement where my cousins' rooms were. The next morning, we got on the road and drove back to Memphis. About three hours after we got back to Memphis, Moses stopped by the house. He and my mother talked as I walked into the living room and sat on the couch.

Moses said his goodbyes and walked out the front door. While my mother was shutting the door, he stepped back in and said, "Oh, I forgot to tell you that last night Ivar's youngest son was murdered."

My mother caught her breath and turned and looked at me. Moses didn't know the relationship that I had with Gaylon, so when he delivered that information, he did it with no knowledge of how I would take it.

I was sitting on the couch, and this was the first time I ever understood what it meant to have an out-of-body experience. I asked him to repeat himself, and he then realized what was happening. We asked what happened. He relayed that Gaylon had been shot in the face and died in the hospital. At the time he was 16 and I was 14. Our birthdays were two days apart, two years apart, and most of my birthdays were celebrated with him. I got up and ran out the front door to the community center. We did not have a phone in the house, so this is where I had to go to make phone calls. The lady who ran the community center was named Jean. She had taken a liking to me, and she told me I was going to be her son. She was an older gay lady. When Jean saw me, she knew something was wrong and immediately let me know that she was there for me. I called home to St. Louis, Gaylon's brother Rod answered the phone. I heard him crying and, in that instant, I knew it was true.

After the call I ran home and lied to my mother about the funeral plans, which prompted us to leave Memphis and head back to St. Louis sooner than we needed to. Rod and Gaylon were like having additional brothers. All their clothes were my hand-me-downs. Their mother was like my second mother, and I spent a lot of my days hanging with them. I found myself at the funeral home looking at him in a casket with a pink teen scarf over his face. They'd used it to cover the bullet hole. This was a major loss to me, and I didn't know how to process what I was feeling at the time. I had just lost my brother, and this was the person that I looked up to. In my eyes he could do no wrong, and now I was faced with the fact that most of the guys in my neighborhood were afraid to turn 16, or at least I was. Sixteen was a common age for guys to be murdered or locked up. There was a strong chance you won't make it past that, but after you make it past sixteen your next concern was making it past age twenty-one. After Gaylon died I decided that I would not allow myself to become attached to a lot of people. In some ways this transition was not a difficult one to make. I moved around so much that I never had time to make longtime friends. It sent me into a light depression for about six months. I started smoking weed heavily, which lasted from ages 14 – 23. We moved back to St. Louis. To this day I'm not sure why, but my mom came home one night and told us to pack. We moved back and stayed in a hotel until we moved in with her best friend Liz. During our stay with Liz, I noticed that my mom began hanging around the guy she called my dad. Liz had a white house with a bedroom she let all five of us stay in. I slept on the floor by the front door.

Once again, I was in school. I started dating a girl in the neighborhood, and every day I would sit on the front porch and wait for her to walk by on her way home from school. I remember telling her how I wished we had never left Memphis. I asked my mom if we could go back. She promised me that at some point we would, but she was working on a few things. I was fed up moving around. I was trying to figure out how to get money.

I started working for her friend who owned the car wash. I would take the money I was making to wash cars and save it so that if my brother and sisters and I needed something to eat I had it stashed under the bed. Some days my mother would be gone all day and she would come back in the evening. For a while it was okay because I realized she was working on something, but when nothing changed, I knew I had to figure something out, because whatever my mother was working on was not working out for my siblings and me.

"Making a hard decision is just like it sounds! If you're a compassionate person it is a task that you wish to pass on, especially if the decision includes people you love and there is a choice that it isn't in their favor. Fifteen years old and that's what I had to do. I had come to a crossroads where I had to decide if I were going to continue to try and be there to help when someone called or if I was going to run for my life and make something happen that would better me. It was far from clear-cut. Things were so bad at that time I was numb and didn't know how to feel about much. It would take a drastic situation for me to decide to step out in the world on my own with very limited resources. It would require me to do something that I rarely like to do, trust people! Fortunately for me, the fear of doing that wasn't as strong as the fear I had of letting the streets take me out. Once I recognized that the people around me were moving in a way that didn't allow them to see what I saw, I knew I had to do something!"

—MARKUS

CHAPTER EIGHT
Label Me A Runaway

"I RAN AWAY FROM home at 15 years old. Partly because my friends were getting killed and my mom had no clue. She was busy dealing with the dude who was supposed to be my father. I realized that if I was ever going to help my family, I had to leave and do something bigger than what was expected of me. I didn't know what that was at the time, but I knew in my heart that it was not staying in St. Louis."
—MARKUS

The day that I left home, Mom had a phone call. Twenty minutes later the guy she said was my father walked in the door, looked at my mother, and asked her to come outside. That was the first time I'd seen him close-up. I followed them out back so I could check on the food that was on the grill. I went back into the house and my mom came in and asked me for the money I was stuffing under the mattress for us. I looked at her with anger and went to give her the money—I think it was about $200. She got it, went outside, and then she came back in with the money I had given her and said that he'd told her to let me keep the money. That made me angry! One, I couldn't believe that she thought that was a kind gesture. This dude had been denying me my whole life, and this was acceptable to her? Two, that was a defining moment for me, and I felt she had chosen a side, and it was not mine.

That night I did not sleep. It was the closest I had ever been to him. I clearly recalled his face, an unfamiliar face of a man who denied my paternity. I could not wrap my mind around the situation. Had he not been present then I would have not taken it to heart, but we were suffering on another level, and once again he was around and not helping. I started remembering all the times we'd barely had food or utilities and the dude would pull up to talk to my mom. If she came back with a few dollars it didn't help much.

There was one time I overheard my mom telling her friend how he said something disrespectful to my little sister, so I waited for him to call, which he did often. I answered the phone and cursed him out. About a week later he pulled up outside of the house and threatened to beat my ass for talking crazy on the phone.

That was the first time I recall seeing him clearly and threatening to beat my ass were the first words he chose to say to me. The man who neglected us and watched us suffer, had the gall to disrespect me. I was the man-child that helped take care of his family. My neighbors across the street heard what happened and came over to check him. They let him know that I was loved on that street. I broke down crying. It was a lot to process. My hate for him was not for me, it was for my mother. In my eyes he had too much control over her and influenced her to make bad decisions regarding us.

The day I left was bittersweet. I was leaving my brother and sisters behind, but as I mentioned earlier, there were two reasons I was leaving other than my mother and father's relationship. I was also leaving because of what was going on with my cousins in the neighborhood.

I had been working at my mom's friend's car wash, and he had told me that he was going to do a tent revival in Chicago. The night before going to the church revival in Chicago, I packed everything I had, which was not much. We had been living on the street, so I didn't have many things to carry. I left with him, without telling my mother. Once we arrived at Chicago, I got out of the car and immediately ran down the street to let my auntie know what was happening. When I got to my auntie's house, we spoke in the kitchen in depth about why I wanted to leave St. Louis. She understood everything I was saying, and she decided that she would make the call to let my mother know of my whereabouts. My mother was on the phone and she was angry. I could stay for a week before she sent me to Minneapolis, Minnesota. She did not tell me why, but I assumed it was because my mother was angry. My aunt did not want to be a part of the situation much longer.

    Running away from home was one of the hardest things I've ever had to do. Leaving my siblings was something I told myself that I wouldn't do. I was always worried about them when I was with them. It wasn't until I had to choose between doing whatever it took to stay alive in St. Louis or taking a chance at leaving with the possibility of being in a better environment where I could do something with myself. I knew if I stayed home that my fate would either be me getting killed or killing someone else. People I was close to had already become victims. I was even around guys whom I personally heard being warned about how close to death they were living. They ignored it, completely blew it off. Seeing that opened my eyes. I didn't want to be one of those guys. Losing Gaylon took away part of my security. When I saw that he could be killed I knew that it could happen to me. It was a weird time for me, my first experience losing someone I practically shared everything with. Looking back, I know that I didn't grieve properly, and I didn't talk to anyone about how I felt. That was when I started looking over my shoulder no matter where I was and who I was with. I did it so much I eventually got numb to the fact that I was gonna die before 21. I had accepted that as my fate. We listened to a lot of Tupac and everything in the music was going on around me, so it was hard not to believe it.

I eventually figured out that if I died no one would be able to help my family. That was my purpose for deciding to fight for my life at that time; otherwise, I think I would have cared less, like many others I knew. It's not like we saw much that made life worth living. When you really look at it, it's a sad situation when a young man is at a point where he's questioning his existence. I'm only touching the surface with my last statement. I think if people really investigated how young Black boys are raised and treated, they would change. It is not an easy thing to accept that at a very young age we are taught to work harder than everybody else. Just like everyone else, we want love and peace.

CHAPTER NINE
Journey for Peace and Love

I LANDED IN MINNEAPOLIS to live with my other aunt. It was a rough welcoming. I was a young kid fresh off the streets of St. Louis. Any older person who knew anything about St. Louis had concerns about me because I was at that age where young boys were known to be active in the streets. When I got to my aunt's house, who I had not seen in two summers, I was ridiculously skinny, and had about 25 dollars in my pocket and damaged hair on my head. I came from an environment where I had experienced everything, I needed to suffer from Post-Traumatic Stress Disorder (PTSD). Along with my aunt were my three cousins and their father in the home. Before coming to live there, I had previously stayed one summer with them, which was one of the best times of my life, so I was extremely happy to be there. This was the aunt that I felt always had my back.

At the time, my uncle was not fond of the idea of me living with them. My aunt did a great job of not letting me know, but I would find out soon. For me to stay, my uncle gave me a rundown of his laws. I had to go to school, get a job, stick to a curfew, and make sure to contribute to the house when I got paid. They were rules I was glad to take on. At first it was harder than I expected. It was the first time I'd lived in a house with a man, and it was the first time I was given that type of structure. Unc was strict on me. He did not just give me those rules; he made sure that I stuck to everything he said. This was so new for me that I had to continually remind myself that naturally boys are supposed to listen to the older guys. He was the man of the house, and that was foreign to me when I typically assumed that role.

In the beginning I felt like he did not like me. Then, after a while, I started noticing that the way he dealt with the family was the way things were supposed to be done. He would get off work, come home, pour a shot of Jim Beam, put an old-school record on his record player, and start cleaning. Then, after cleaning up, he would start dinner. To me, it was the most amazing, life changing experience. To this day I can remember how the whole atmosphere would change when he was present. I loved it! It was the first time I realized that I had not felt safe at any time before that. Unc was my role model, the man who I feel instilled a lot in me. Watching him helped usher me properly into manhood. As time went on, he and I grew close. He became so cool that I looked forward to him asking me to do things for him. He was the first guy to ever show me how to put a crease in my jeans, edge the front lawn, and plant grass seeds. Watching my uncle standing in the mirror shaving gave me the feeling of what I thought it would be like to have a father at home. I guess it's also because I saw that in the movies.

Our fishing trips were some of the most memorable moments of my life. I remember one time we went fishing for 30 days straight. The funny thing is before we got to this point, he had put me out twice and asked me to leave for good once I got my daughter's mom pregnant. I had to respect his stance.

Before the pregnancy happened, he continuously warned me that I was too in love, and I had not gotten my life all the way together yet. I tried to hide the news from my aunt and uncle once I found out, but somehow, they knew. One day I came home from school and my aunt was in the basement on the computer. She asked me to come take a seat, then she sat on the weight bench that was sitting in the middle of the room. I should have known then that something was up. They were disappointed in me, especially my aunt. She knew my life had been turbulent and she was trying to provide me a way to do better. They saw this as another setback for me, and rightfully so. My uncle eventually asked me to leave because what I had done was against the example he was trying to set for my cousins. It made sense to me. Babies having babies was an epidemic in our community, and I had just added another stereotypical statistic to my name. I ended up leaving to move with a friend of mine most of the time. When I wasn't staying with my friend, I stayed in random places.

Once again, I was out on the streets trying to find my way. Once again, I started questioning the existence of God. I did not understand how my heart was always in the right place, yet it seemed like nothing would ever go right for me, but I kept my faith. I believed that if I just could survive and not die in the streets, I would one day turn this shit around. One of my favorite singers wrote a song called, "Looking for Love." This song is one of the reasons I was able to deal with a lot of bs. It reminded me that at some point I would find the guidance I needed. Part of me wanted to be angry at everyone that I felt turned their back on me or did not notice that I was worth keeping around. Looking back, I think this is why I fell so hard for my daughter's mother. She was the first to make me feel loved. I vowed that I would not hold grudges against people.

Unforgiveness, especially of my mother, made my pain worse, and I could not handle that again. Forgiving people made it easier for me to move forward without allowing those emotions to mess up something unrelated. It was difficult enough going day to day, pushing myself, trying to figure out what I was going to do with my life. I also fought to believe that there was some good somewhere in the world.

From 1992 – 1998, there was a lot of instability in my life. I had to gain some self-control, because I was trying to share my story to anyone who would listen. I did not understand that either no one believed I dealt with all that I had, or they had problems of their own. In the streets, bros don't talk or care about your shit unless you vibe. I learned to live in my head and have my own back.

I began to understand that I was a sensitive guy. I cared. I cared about people and I cared about life. I had to bury the idea that God felt sorry for me and was going to send someone to come, validate my pain and make things better. That was something I picked up from going to church. The reality was that I had work to do. Yeah, God was going to help, but I had to start making decisions. I sat myself down and came to the harsh reality that I had started on a bumpy road while under the supervision of someone else and along the way I had adopted a certain belief system and started operating within that belief system which kept me on my current path.

It all overlapped. I had missed my mark. I had the chance to use the help my aunt was giving and stick to the plan--honestly, I should have ended up at least graduating high school and going to college. The decisions I made forced their hand. I habitually made emotional decisions.

For the first time ever, I was living in a dope neighborhood, I had stability, a few dollars, time, and freedom. I chose to use all that to look for something I felt like I missed: a childhood. I was out looking for love, hanging with friends, and going to parties. I was all typical teenager stuff, but I was not in that position. I was operating at a deficit having lived a deficient life. Those are the things you do when you're not trying to convince some older people that although you come from a bad city, you're not bad, and they shouldn't worry about you. I didn't bring any trouble to the house, but I did get kicked out of the public-school system.

The funny thing is that I was kicked out of school for joking with the wrong principal. I made a simple joke about wanting to go to an alternative school and she made it happen the next day. Big mistake on my behalf. Looking back, I think it was an accumulation of the things she heard about me, and me skipping class to go rap at lunch did not help.

By the time I entered school in Minneapolis, I had been out so long I was there just so I could feel like a normal kid. I had stopped seeing value in school in elementary. I don't even remember having a year where I didn't get in a fight or argue with a teacher. Being poor, you find ways to get the fuck out of class, so you don't have to be that name on the sheet of paper that everyone is passing around and laughing about. That happened to me in junior high. I went to school with drug dealers and my clothing game was already so-so; I could not compete. I did not sell drugs regularly until I quit high school. I had a close friend who taught me the game and introduced me to a Jamaican guy who I bought my stuff from. I only started because my daughter was on the way and I did not have money or a stable place to live.

When people say the road to hell is paved with good intentions, that is real. If your good thoughts are not followed with proper actions to get the desired outcome, then in the real world your intentions do not exist. Results matter, especially in the real world. It took me a while to understand this. One reason is you must be aware in advance that you can't control other people's reactions to whatever it is you're presenting. Approaching things that way kept me with a real sense of how I should deal.

For me there was power in having my own back. I stopped expecting anything from people, which minimized the number of times I was disappointed. Then I started paying more attention to the way people around me moved. It became easy to tell at what level I could trust them. I realized that I had to trust myself and stay in my own lane if I wanted different results from my actions.

One thing I learned from watching my mom was that, although she was a parent and had the responsibilities of taking care of her kids, it did not take away whatever previous situations or personal feelings she had toward life. There are things people experience personally regardless of their status. Many of us walk around dealing with the effects, some of us look for solutions, some do not, some people aren't aware that they have issues. My mom's parenting style was partially driven by her perception of life, her personal fears, and her ability to ration.

I would listen to my mom reminisce with her friends about her past and her upbringing, I noticed her feelings about her past. Honestly, it was a bit shocking to me when I first caught on to how she felt and how intense some of those feelings were. In our house we did not discuss our feelings often. My mom loved us, and she tried hard to sustain a stable life for us, however I grew to understand that she was fighting more than one battle at the same time. Most of what she was fighting was outside the house, out in the world, and when she came home, I would see her trying to smile and be mom while in deep thought.

When we were at our worst, my mother and I began working like teammates. The days we would sleep in the car, we would plan the day together. She was extremely strong, and although she was stressed out and disappointed in herself, she would hide it. My siblings were unaware, but I was. I would try and ignore the moments she would lash out at me. I fully understood that life had not been fair to her. A single mother of six, no income, and homeless. This was not how she saw herself. My mom was a dreamer. During her time in the military, she traveled internationally, she then would come home and share her experiences with us.

In the beginning, as most children are, I was taught to do what I was told and that was it, but in my case with the need for me to help with my grandmother, people started interacting with me differently. The way I was given information was on a higher level than someone would talk to a normal five-year-old. Alzheimer's and its effects had to be explained to me. Once my grandmother moved to Texas to be cared for by my aunt, my mother then needed my help with my siblings. I then became their caretaker as well.

From what I know, my mom had a rough life. A single black woman, making a low income and dealing with the pressure of society, her kids, and trying to maintain a sense of self. I saw her deal with it all, and as her sidekick, I felt bad that I was too young to help her. I saw the anger and disappointment it brought out. I remember her frustration when being denied loans after realizing we didn't have enough money for food and utilities. Seeing my mom in pain like that was traumatizing, but no matter what choices she made, I found a way to understand why. When I got older and started dating, the women I dated helped me see some of the things I think my mom was struggling with. It helped me realize that she was trying to do what she considered her best, and I love her for trying to hold on to us. Through all her mistakes, she never let go, no matter what!

Although I was around people all the time, I felt alone. It seemed like I was living out certain moments only so I could learn a lesson of how I didn't fit in. My way of thinking never seemed to coincide with the people around me. For instance, there were times when I skipped school with friends and everyone wanted to go drink, get high, and sleep with chicks. We would go to a house where everything was set up and happening. While in that environment I would try and start a conversation about how we could be more productive with our time. Nobody was trying to hear that. The girls around me would start ignoring me when I started talking like that. I was a heavy thinker, the weed enhanced that. I admit I was somewhat paranoid because I was aware of the possible negative outcomes that could happen to us after experiencing the tragedy of death around me. I just knew that I wanted more than what I was currently experiencing. I knew that I wanted, hell, deserved a better life.

Did I know exactly what that more was? No. I did know when we were doing things that would not pay off in the end as we grew into manhood Most of the time, I would make an excuse to leave to avoid feeling and looking awkward. I was confused and I tried to decipher what pulled at me and caused me to overthink as I maneuvered through my environment. Looking back, I understand now. Some places are exactly meant for us. Sometimes we end up in places we don't belong because we are under the guidance of someone else or we make a choice to be there thinking that's what we want. I'm no stranger to that. Many times, I put myself in situations because I thought that is what I was supposed to do and quickly found out that I had fucked up. After so long I started realizing that I needed a close mentor or a role model. I wasn't thinking of those titles exactly, but you get the point.

CHAPTER TEN
My Role Model

ALTHOUGH UNC AND I had a rocky start, he turned out to be the best role model I ever had. Living with him and my aunt was the first time I lived in a two-parent home. In my eyes their home was perfect. I had never been a part of a family that operated the way that things did there. Together they sat down and did the monthly bills and budget. My aunt owned two companies that my uncle worked for, that too was different. My uncle was a man, more importantly, he was the man of his house. It did not matter that he worked for my aunt. They worked together as a team within their household. His role as protector and provider was solid, and that is how he operated in his house. I witnessed how two people could build if they worked together. Friday nights were my favorite; it was family night. As I mentioned earlier, my uncle would come home from work, put on his old-school records, the vinyl albums, then clean up the house before preparing dinner. If I was home, I was required to help clean. Once everyone was home from school, he would have us all come to the living room and watch movies. That was very different for me. That was the quality time I had always craved.

Mentally it took time to adjust to everything. I was so used to life moving fast and unexpected tragedy happening at any moment. I was more afraid of good and happy things because they didn't seem real. The existence of bad things was my truth and reality. I was conflicted because I wanted to experience good so bad but when it came,

I did not feel deserving. Probably because I had never done anything specifically for myself, and I didn't grow up where I was made to feel special in any way. At that point I had one, maybe two birthday parties. The birthdays that I did celebrate besides the one Charlie, my mom's boyfriend, threw for me was my cousin Gaylon's birthdays, and his mom would invite me to the celebration. Now that Gaylon was gone, I had no care for the future birthdays.

I began to admire my uncle. No one had ever paid as much attention to me as he did, other than my Uncle Gene, whom I didn't get much time with due to drugs and him passing before I was old enough to really learn from him. I remember Unc teaching me to shave and make a bed. Looking back, it was like being in the military. He would go behind me after I cleaned up to make sure I did it right. In the beginning of me being at the house I think he was tough on me until he realized I was not a bad kid. The days we would go fishing were some of the greatest days of my life. We would be there all day and he would tell me stories about his childhood. He was not afraid to show emotion and talk about the way he felt in each of the situations he experienced. That helped me tremendously. I was still impressionable and trying to figure out how to deal with my feelings.

It was rare for me to have someone to ask how I felt or if I was okay. I always thought that was strange especially because I was going through an avalanche of bad situations. I barely got hugs or heard the words I love you from anyone. I hated that because I would see my friends hug and kiss their parents or grandparents, and I didn't have that type of affection. I made it through that by telling myself that I wasn't supposed to worry about being loved at that point and time; it would come one day from somewhere. Plus, I felt guilty expecting my mom to pay me attention when she had other kids to tend to and she had to deal with us barely having anything. One thing I could not understand was how she was able to continue a relationship with the man she said was my father knowing he always denied us.

My awareness was sometimes my tormentor. I witnessed the dysfunction around me and became painfully aware that my mom was in a relationship with a man, who she claimed to be my father, but did not want a relationship with me nor my siblings. This perplexed me to the point of aggravation. I remember asking her to stop allowing this man to come to our home. She never stopped it. I remember many times he would come by and pick her up on days we did not have utilities on in the house or food. I hated them both. This guy owned multiple businesses and drove nice cars, yet we lived in abject poverty without basic needs met. I think she hoped for the day he would accept us, so she continued to be around him, but in the end, it did more damage that good. I felt like she chose him over us. The final offense was when we had to deal with her anger after he did whatever it was and sent her home.

I wish I had taken advantage of the opportunity to be happy my aunt and uncle provided for me. They gave me a safe place to live in a good environment. I did not do what I was supposed to do when it came to school. I was accustomed to instability. It was normal to me. I did not know what good things to expect from the life I was living at the time. I have lived in so many houses that I just knew something was going to go wrong and I would not be able to stay.

What I know now is that if anything went wrong, it was partly because I expected it to. It's easy to get caught up in your own world when you make yourself believe that a lot of people don't understand you. I expected people to judge me and always perceive things the wrong way. I know my aunt was not happy when she found out that I was kicked out of high school. No matter what, she had always supported me ever since I can remember. I had been out of school so long I really did not know how to be a student. While sitting in class I used to look around and judge a lot of the kids, thinking that their lives must be easy. I also felt they judged me as well. I felt like they were all looking at me judging me as I adjusted from being on the streets.

It did not take me long to become well-known at the school. I was a popular freshman. It was the first time I had been to a school that diverse. Everybody seemed to get along and I hung out with all types of crowds. Unfortunately, my heart was not at school. My family back home in St. Louis dominated my thoughts and I found it difficult to fully concentrate on school. I knew that when I called home, which was frequently I would hear the silent struggle in my mother's voice. I knew that I would hear the pain in the pauses of each word she spoke. This was my preoccupation, my distraction that caused me the inability to focus on grades, attendance, and homework. My heart was in St. Louis struggling with the family I loved and left behind. That made it hard to see myself staying in school for years trying to pursue a degree. I imagined that I would be able to follow another path to accomplish my grand goal of helping my family out of poverty. I believed, at the time that, the only way this would be accomplished is if I did not have to be in school all day. That was not a smart way to think, but it is what my young mind believed.

After I was kicked out of the public-school system, I had to go to the alternative school. It was then that I made the final decision that school was no longer for me and that I needed to get my GED. I stopped going to school and started hustling and working my job. I ended up having to quit my job because I was standing at the counter and I was afraid that the police were watching me due to my hustling career, so I left the job at the grocery store where I was very visible and returned to my old job at the malt shop to work as a dishwasher.

At the time I was a heavy weed smoker, and it made me paranoid. It was never confirmed that the police or anyone else was watching me. I felt exposed and vulnerable, so I took extra precautions to protect myself. It seemed like every time I would get high, I would start to worry about what life was going to be like in the future, I became anxiety ridden. I remember one day I was smoking. I was lying in bed and I started thinking about all the bad things people said about me. The negative thoughts replayed in my mind like a bad soundtrack. The soundtrack in my mind reminded me that I was a bad father, I was a bum, the list was endless. I was thinking of all the homes I'd been kicked out of and the many times I had no one to help me. This day may have been my catalyst for change. Oddly inspired, I got up right then, ironed my clothes, took a shower, got dressed, and told myself I was going to go early in the morning to look for jobs. After I got completely dressed, I looked in the mirror and realized how high I was. I looked at the clock, it was 3:30 in the morning. I had at least four hours before I could make my way to look for jobs. For me, smoking was something that helped me see clearly that the path I was on was not going to help me achieve my goals. Although I was high that night and was being somewhat ridiculous, it was in those moments that I knew I had to change my life, or I was not going to be able to help my family.

I was in a bad place mentally. I was low and kept crumbling but was still trying to find some type of resolution. My daughter, her mother, and I grew up in poverty and all the atrocities that come with it. I wanted to change her life, my life, but more importantly I wanted to provide a better life for the life that she and I had created. My dreams back then surpassed my logic. Looking back, I understand now that my way of thinking was the way to rise out of the struggle. But I was not in a place where I could make that happen. I wanted success so bad that I got the bright idea that if I went to LA that I could completely change my life in a year, and that would help us.

Once I got to LA, life wasn't what I expected. My aunt had a house full of children. My cousin's friends also lived with them, so when

I got there, I had to find a place to sleep in the house. My cousin's friends weren't so happy because I walked in the door ready to start changing things. I was on a mission, and I knew I had to get back to my daughter, and the only way to do that was to make sure I had money coming in the door. My aunt and uncle owned the building of a club and he had a pager shop. My uncle had made a name for himself in LA. He was successful, but he ended up going to prison. I spoke with my aunt, and she gave me permission to do whatever I needed to for the family.

First, I asked all my cousin's friends to move out of the house and allow the girls to have more space to be alone. My aunt put me back in school and I was bumped to 11th grade. She enrolled me at Dorsey High School. I made the basketball and the football team, but I did not get to play. I didn't last in the school long at all. Within the first week of being there I got into an argument with a player on the football team. I found out that his stepfather was well known. He let me know that if I stayed at the school and if I wanted to be protected, I would have to be down with them. I told him I was from St. Louis and that I did not need anyone to protect me. Later that day I walked outside the school and there were about 40 guys waiting outside to fight me all from the jungle, a neighborhood in LA. I stayed in the school until my cousin picked me up. Lucky for me, he knew many of them. The next day, my Aunt Janie and I had to go up to the school and the principal felt it was not safe for me to stay in the school. They suggested that she enroll me at LA High. While at LA High I made the basketball team, but once again, I did not stay long. This was my last attempt at school, and afterward I completely quit. I knew, however, that I had to do something productive and life sustaining, so my cousin and I reopened my uncle's pager shop. I needed to earn money to support my daughter and to help my younger cousins I was living with.

Again, I started selling marijuana, and this time I was doing well enough to make sure bills were paid at the house. Upstairs from the pager shop was a huge space with rooms and since my family owned the building, we turned the upstairs into a club. Things started turning around. We started doing parties, and it would be packed. People were still buying pagers from us, so we had double income at the time. We brought attention to ourselves and a guy came by and told us that we would not be allowed to stay open if the guys in the hood did not get a piece of the profit. We denied them, which resulted in a big shooting on the busiest night we ever had. We took a big hit, and our parties stopped. Not long after that one of our friends was killed on Crenshaw and Stocker in front of the Magic Johnson Movie Theaters. That was the final blow and my cousin and I were pretty much back to ground zero. After our business venture failed and KB passed, I knew that I had to leave LA. I was afraid that if I did not, I would not make it out of that city alive.

I returned to Minneapolis after being away for a year. Once I got back, I found myself in the same position I was when I left. This was disheartening. I moved in with my friend and went back to my old job at the grocery store. I ran into another close friend of mine and we began selling weed again. However, this time I had a plan.

One thing I learned in LA was how to put a plan together and execute it fully. I had never done that. Also, while living in LA, I saw how lavish life could be. I wanted it. Although, choosing to hustle again was not the best decision, it was a decision I made as part of my larger plan. Once again, unfortunately, I was noticed by some guys I wish I could have avoided. Then again, I don't think they had any control in the part they played in what I am about to tell you.

One morning, not long after my return to Minneapolis, I woke up to a message. It was not a typical message. It was a message I heard in my spirit, and I believe came from God. This was the first time I had this kind of experience. I felt the message clear and deep in my spirit. I heard in my spirit as I prepared to start my day, that I was going to go through something unavoidable that day and that I should not panic. The message perplexed me, yet I continued.

I got dressed and went to the bus stop headed to work to go pick up my check. I heard one of my best friends whistle while he was getting off of a different bus. The first thing he said to me was that the day seemed gloomy, and he had a feeling that somebody he knew was going to get something. His comment scared me; we both knew what that something was. Although he said this, and I heard what I heard earlier, I did not tell him what I had experienced earlier. Together we went to my job and picked up my check. We decided to walk 20 blocks to his house which was close to my daughter's mother's house. After I stopped with him at his house, I continued to walk to my daughter's mother's house alone. While walking I came across the bridge, I could see about three blocks down two guys walking out of a house on the right side of the street. On the left side of the street there were three guys in the alley. In my mind and spirit, I knew this was the situation I had been warned about.

Once I got to the middle of the bridge I tried to turn around, but I had no control over my legs. It was the most terrifying thing ever. I did not understand what was happening. As I walked, I got about a block away from the guys when they noticed me. I continued walking, and by this time all the guys were on the left side of the street.

As I became parallel to them, one of the guys crossed the street, and walked over to me. He asked me who I knew in the neighborhood. I could hear a voice telling me not to say a name. I said a name anyway. I said my girl's dad's name because I knew he was known in the neighborhood.

Seconds later, the guy pulled a gun out, put it to my head, and said to empty my pockets. Right after that, two cars were coming down the street, so he put the gun down. At that time, I was contemplating hitting him and trying to run, but by then the other guys came across the street and put two guns in my back. The main guy started digging in my pockets. One guy went through the notebook I was carrying. The head dude started asking me where the drugs were! I had never seen that before and I asked him what he was talking about. The guy asked me again for the drugs, and after he realized I didn't have anything, he told the other guys to take me up the hill into the alley so he could shoot me.

Now, by this time we were standing outside in front of the library which wasn't a full block away from my daughter's house. While the guys were trying to drag me up the hill to the back of the library, I could see my daughter's bedroom window to the left very clear. I started to ask the guys what they wanted, and I kept asking them to let me go.

One guy asked, "Why?" and I said, "Cuz, I don't have anything else to give you. Can you let me go?"

The guy told me to shut up and don't say the word "cuz" anymore. The main dude told his guys to take me in the alley because he was going to kill me. I said, "If you're going to kill me then let me go say bye to my daughter!"

They were looking like I was crazy, but honestly the whole time in my head I could hear something telling me not to panic. All I heard in my head was, "Don't panic! Don't panic!" I did not feel afraid, I didn't understand why. My life was about to end!

Again, I said "cuz" while talking, and the smallest guy hit me in the face. When he hit me in the face my automatic response was to grab him. When I reached for him, the guy with the gun hit me in the face and he split my left eye. The other guy ran, it was at that moment that I was able to get away. I ran across the street and continued running until something told me to stop and turn around. I stopped and turned around. I crossed back over to the other side of the street and started walking toward the guy, who was now standing at the corner pointing the gun at me. I told the guy that if he was going to shoot me that he was going to shoot me in my face. I put my jacket from over my head that was covered with blood. The guy looked at me and looked back, but he did not see anyone. He looked at me again, but this time he did not look back. As he talked, he noticed two little boys walking out of the library's front door. He then turned around and ran. I noticed that I was standing at the gate in front of my daughter's house as I saw him running away. I walked through the gate and pressed the doorbell. When my daughter's mom came to the door, she saw the blood on my face and started screaming and yelling. She immediately took me upstairs to clean my face. While explaining the situation to her, I heard the doorbell ring. I could hear the two little boys asking if I was okay. I did not go down to see them. These boys, whether they knew or not, had saved my life.

Looking back, the only thing I can think is that it was God showing me that he was real. He showed me how I needed to focus back on him and that he had me. Regardless of my current state, God proved to me that He was my protector. To this day I still think about the situation, and I'll go to my grave trying to better understand, what happened, why it happened, and how God protected me. After that near death experience, my daughter's mother and I talked. I decided that I would go to St. Louis, get a job, and find us a home. Once again, I was leaving, thinking that I was going to make my life better, unaware that I was continuing the habit of instability.

I returned to St. Louis, and I was on a mission. I stayed between my friend's and my sister's home. I finally decided I was going to stick with the GED process and take the test, but then I got hired at McDonald's and Sonic. I eventually started working at a gas station near my sister's apartment. While working at the gas station, I met a man who owned a few properties in the area. He was reluctant to rent to me because of my age, but over time we became cool and he rented me my first home. I prayed every day and hid myself from everyone so I could cry. I was tired! I lost the desire to smoke weed to numb my pain. I was tired of being around other struggling people who were just as confused as I was. My GED came in the mail the same week I got the keys to the house. I had a double celebration of momentary joy. Not only was I moving into my first home, but I also passed the GED. I then sent for my daughter and her mom. We stayed in St. Louis for about a year, she was ready to leave after that first year. It was hard on her. We were 18 and 19 years old trying to live the family life, all the while she was getting a closer glimpse at some of the struggles my life came with while being in St. Louis. I came home from work one day and she was packing the house. I asked what was going on and she told me she was leaving with or without me.

She ended up telling me that my cousins and their mother had been in her ear the whole time she lived in St. Louis. They were telling her that I wouldn't be able to take care of her properly, and if she wanted to move in with them, she could. After hearing this, I believed everything that came out of her mouth. At that moment I realized all the signs I had ignored. I thought that keeping my family in church was going to help us, but I had taken her around the wrong people. The only thing that shocked me was I was completely blindsided; I had no idea that all that was going on under my nose. So many traps this world has for us. Here I was 20 years old, finally in a place where I could see my life about to change. I had a family that I loved more than life and I sabotaged myself by trusting people.

I had to make a firm decision that day. I refused to let them leave without me. By the end of the week, we were in a U-Haul driving back to Minnesota. Once again, I was on the move, but this time I thought my life was finally coming together.

This time was better than the other because we were together. We moved in with her dad and stepmom until I got us a nice place about 10 minutes away. I did not see it coming, but I was losing her. I would find out within a year of being back in Minnesota.

Leaving St. Louis with my then girlfriend and my daughter, I learned the importance of keeping good-hearted, and supportive people around you. Those who spoke ill of me while my daughter and her mom lived in St. Louis, do not know that I know what they did behind my back. I made a big mistake taking my daughter and her mother into an environment where I had jealous adult family members who did not believe in my ability to provide and care for my family. For some reason they chose to spread that message and interfere in the relationship of two teenage parents who were just trying to figure it out. This started a lot of frustration and confusion between her and me. It took us 15 years after our breakup to be able to talk about what happened. Fortunately, life has brought us to a place where we have mutual respect. What I'm going to explain isn't to paint a negative picture of either one of us, but to tell my story and through my story explain the plight of an unguided teenage parent.

Some of the happiest days of my life were with my daughter and her mom. That type of love was celestial. When my daughter was born, I knew that no matter what happened in my life, if she were with me, there was nothing that could stop me. I would take her to the basketball court and sometimes in the middle of the game she would walk out on the court just to get a kiss. I thought that was so dope! She made me feel like a king. When at home, I'd be in the bathroom and she'd walk to the door and sing Beyonce's "Speechless." I felt like my heart was literally walking outside of my body. To this day she is my greatest accomplishment. I was oblivious to life for a moment. I had my family, but it was not strong enough to make it through life's hardships. We were young and trying to do our best. It all ended because of our immaturity. My daughter's mother back then was my best friend. She was the person who fed me and put dollars in my pocket when I was on the street.

I moved my family into an apartment near Richfield in south Minneapolis. Currently, I was 21 and my daughter was 3 years old. Things with me and her mom were rocky at times, but I was happy that we had our own place again. For me, the hard part was trying to figure out how to take care of my family. We had a nice home, but I like to get ahead and not live paycheck to paycheck. I was now back in Minneapolis jobless, with a family, and bills. I signed up to work for a temp agency and went through the process of trying one job out and moving on to the next.

One job experience that I will never forget was when I worked as a temporary worker at a print shop. I worked there for two weeks. Older White guys who made stereotypical jokes about me daily were my co-workers. I wanted to leave that job the first time it happened, but I knew that would affect my family. The beginning of the second week I was asked about my education. When the workers found out I had not graduated, they complained to the manager, who decided to fire me. In his words, I didn't seem enthusiastic about the job. I hated those jobs; they were depressing. My life unfolded before me like an old-school movie where the Black guy couldn't afford to feed his family. I knew I was supposed to be doing something better than what I was doing then. I had a great job in St. Louis before coming back to Minneapolis, so that fact did not help my emotional, nor my mental well-being at the time. I was an overthinker and put major pressure on myself because I wanted to make sure my daughter and her mom had everything they needed. We lived in a nice place, in a decent neighborhood, but we did not have a car. I judged myself about not having a car. I was becoming more self-conscious because I wasn't dressing well. After paying bills, I had nothing left. I was 21 with what I thought were failed old man problems.

Soon my daughter's mom and I began to argue seemingly about everything. I started working more to get extra money to buy better stuff for her, hoping that would help us. Looking back, that was not smart. Things got worse, and then she stopped bringing my daughter home, until finally, she stopped coming home too. I knew she was over me, but I did not understand why. She told me that I wanted too much in life too soon and that she was a simple person. I knew that about her, and that is what made me love her the way I did. But I was also very ambitious. We were engaged, but that seemed to no longer be important. Once I found out she had a new boyfriend, I knew that I had lost all respect. What a hard pill to swallow. In my head I was trying hard to make things better for us, but that may have been part of the problem. It was never clear to me what I was not doing that she needed me to do. On the final day of our relationship, I was sitting on the couch watching a competition show and holding my daughter. My daughter's mom came in and started watching with us. A guy on the TV took his shirt off and she immediately yelled and started talking about how sexy he was. This added more aggravation to our strained relationship. I knew about her secret relationship, so I got mad and asked her not to do that in front of my daughter.

She got pissed, got up and grabbed her coat, and went to the neighbor's house. When she got there, I called and she hung up, but moments later, she pocket-dialed me and I heard her telling the neighbors how sick of me she was. Something snapped in me. I got up, took my daughter into the bedroom, and I prayed. I then took my daughter to her aunt, grabbed my GED and walked out.

First, I called my daughter's grandfather. He and I were close, and I respected his advice. He was aware that I had lost the respect of the people around me. He advised me to go back to school and continue writing. To comfort me, he told me that while I attended school, he would care for my daughter until I was able to come back around. I promised him that no matter what happened, I would always take care of my family. However, at the time, I did not think the breakup would be as bad as it was, but I found that I was wrong. To make matters worse, neither he nor I knew that he would die within a year of our conversation. Fortunately, we kept in touch until 3, maybe 4 weeks before he went to the hospital.

I went to my Aunt Faith to talk to her that night. We called my other aunt in Chicago, who suggested that I come there and go to college. Before leaving for Chicago, my Aunt Faith told me that she would take her hat off to me if I ever make it to be somebody in this life. It would take me about 10 years to understand what she said to me.

Staying with my aunt in Chicago confirmed one thing and proved another thing to me. It confirmed I was on my own, and it proved that I was at a place in my life that I should not expect sympathy from anyone. When I arrived, I was heartbroken. I had lost my girl and at the time I was not able to talk to my daughter. Every night I had nightmares. I would see them both in the room with me; once I saw them both in the room with me and I reached out! I found out that didn't just happen in the movies. It took about a month before I could finish a full plate of food and my hair fell out. Once again, I wanted to give up, but now I knew that I couldn't; I had to do something with my life. Just days before the madness of our breakup, I was playing with my daughter, making her sing Beyonce's Speechless to me. Now, I sat alone and pondered my sadness. I did not know who she was around or what was going on in her life.

My experience with my aunt was not what I thought it would be. One day I went to Malcolm X College to try and talk to the basketball coach about getting on the team, not realizing I was in one of the biggest basketball colleges in the city. The only basketball background I had was one year in high school. The coach would not talk to me, so I figured I'd hang out in the gym until their practice was over. At the time I was a jumper, so I kept jumping and sticking my arm in the rim. There was an older guy in the stands who was sitting and watching. After the practice was over, the coach ignored me. The other guy, who had been watching me from the stands, called me over and invited me to try out for his team at Kennedy King College. I went to the Kennedy King tryout. I did not do as well as I wanted to, but he told me that I had heart and had a good work ethic, he told me that he would help me out.

I became deeply depressed. I was unprepared for it. For one, it was something I'd never had a conversation about. There are no words that compare to that type of emotional pain. I think mine may have been worse because I had to accept the fact that I was failing at life and I had recently lost my family. It took my appetite and zeal for life away. I was consistently having nightmares, and I couldn't make it through the days without damn near breaking down. Luckily, I had a lady friend from St. Louis who lived in Chicago who I started spending time with. Well, it was more like she was nursing me back to health. At one point she had to drag me out of the bed, force me to eat, make sure I exercised, and then take me to basketball practice. This lasted almost a full month before I was able to get my wits about myself. Once I finally started moving around again, I started making plans. Although now I was having trouble getting to my daughter, I knew I would eventually get there, and I needed to have my stuff together.

Change is scary, but I became accustomed to it. Change can take away whatever security you think you have. Looking back, I looked at change from a negative perspective, instead of an opportunity to grow. I moved around so much in my life that I began to wish for stability. I did not want to move again. I wanted a place where I could stay and have consistent friends in a consistent environment. The type of change I experienced left me traumatized. My perspective would have been different if we moved out of our home into a bigger home in a better neighborhood. That would have been a positive change. That, however, had not been my perspective.

After I tried out for the basketball team, the coach decided to keep me around. For a couple weeks I went to practice, as well as basketball camps. Returning home from a basketball camp one day, my aunt asked me when I was moving out. I told her I was planning to move soon and asked if she wanted me to leave that day. She said yes, so I packed my things and left. I called my coach, and he found another player who let me stay with him. I stayed with Keith for about two months. During that time, Coach Dildy took me to other basketball camps. Eventually he invited a college coach from a school in Milwaukee called Cardinal Stritch to come to an exhibition game he sponsored. I had a great game that day and was offered a partial scholarship to play at the school.

CHAPTER ELEVEN

Milwaukee

I NEVER IMAGINED THAT I would attend college. The basketball team was at a nice school, but to me it was a miracle. When I arrived at the school on move day, my name was written on a paper basketball that was taped to the door. It was like a dream, a dream come true. I was shocked. I played one year of basketball in my whole life. It was surreal the first two weeks of school. I slept in my clothes every night because I just knew something was going to go wrong. I figured they would realize they had the wrong person and would rescind their offer. Cardinal Stritch was an amazing experience. I made a lot of international friends and the coach took us on a trip to Europe.

Going to Europe was a culture shock. It changed my life walking in London, walking in Paris, taking a train to Germany, and playing basketball in places like Belgium. Even the restaurants were amazing. The experience was like nothing I could have imagined. Paris and Germany were two of my favorite places. One day after leaving a castle in the countryside of Germany, we were riding the bus down the back road and I looked out at the green grass and I felt this overwhelming feeling. It was something spiritual, and to this day I believe this was the moment where I changed as a person. I felt good.

We took a boat across the English Channel. I remember looking out at the water and smiling to myself. I felt like for the first time I had done something major, something worth bragging about. Something to be proud of as a man. I could not wait to get back and share my trip with my mother. Although she and I weren't on the best terms, I called her anyway to let her know that I was in school. I wanted her to be proud of me. I knew that when she was in the military, part of her tour was in Germany. I called to talk to her about the things I had seen in the bars that I went to. I was 23 years old and a freshman in college.

When I returned home from Europe, I got a phone call from my daughter's mother. She asked me if I wanted to be back in my daughter's life. I told her yes, and she suggested that I move back to Minneapolis so we could co-parent. I had a hard decision to make. The coach had spoken to me and told me that I would be team captain the next season. I wanted to be back with my daughter badly. My commitment to be her father was more important to me than anything; I didn't care about any of the other stuff.

A few months before going to Europe we did a clinical at Marquette University where I met a coach from Minneapolis at a school in Order Hills. I reached out to the coach in Minneapolis and told him I was returning to the city and I would like to play basketball. The college invited me to come to the school. Once I returned to Minneapolis, I got a job at the SA gas station and moved back into my basement apartment.

Within a month of being back in Minneapolis, I saw my daughter only twice. Things did not go as planned, so I did not stay long. I quit school and moved back to St. Louis, still missing my daughter.

One day I was lying on my mom's couch when I got a call from my coach in Chicago. He asked me why I had made the moves that I had. I told him that I did it all for my daughter, and I thought things would work out for the better for both her and me. He was disappointed in me because he had advised me to get my degree and get on my own two feet, before I did anything else. He reminded me that I came a long way to end up back where I started. He stressed that I needed to figure out what my next move was.

The following week I got up and went down to Harris Stowe State University and signed up for classes. I was 26 years old living in a college dorm. I had just given up the best thing that ever happened to me, but I was okay with it because I was trying to get closer to my daughter. I made the basketball team and became a student orientation leader, which allowed me to have dinner with the Governor at the Governor's mansion. I joined an organization called Hundred Black Men Collegiate 100. I was still trying to find out what I wanted to do with my life. I was unsure. But I was back in the city with my family on the other side of town, and everything was a little better than it had been the last time I was home.

One day during my history class, the professor told us that we would all have to do a documentary to pass the class. I had never done a documentary, nor had I edited a shot, or anything related to film. He put us in teams of three, but the other two people on my team quit school at the same time, so I no longer had teammates. I asked my professor if I still had to do a documentary. He told me yes if I wanted to pass the class. After choosing my topic, St. Louis public housing, I started spending time in the media lab to learn how to edit iMovie software. I then bought a camera from school and went around the store shooting. I found out that I liked shooting with the camera. I liked it so much that I went to my coach and quit the basketball team so I could spend more time in the lab with highlight tapes. And shooting videos with the guys that stayed on campus. One day while at the club with my friends, I saw a guy walking around with a camera. I noticed every time I went to the club; the same guy was at most of the clubs. After I finished my documentary, I walked up to him, handed him my horrible documentary, and asked him if he would teach me what he knew. About a month later I checked my and saw that he had invited me to work on the rapper "Chingy's" music video. He told me I was working for him as a production assistant. I did not know what that was, but I was okay with it. I was a Production Assistant (PA) on Murphy Lee's last music video for Universal Records. I got close with the Assistant Director, Sunni Powell, and we stayed in touch throughout the years. For the next three years I worked at the juvenile detention center in the daytime, at night I would shoot club promos and music videos. One day I went into a club across the street from the college dorms, and I met a guy named Yomi Martin. Yomi turned out to be one of the owners of Apple Bottom Jeans. The day we met he asked me who I worked for and I told him nobody. He told me to call him tomorrow because he had a job for me. The next day I met him at a kids' activity center for his youngest son's birthday. I shot the video, edited it, and sent it back to him. He loved it so much that he told me he wanted me to work for the summer at his company. To my surprise he hired me to fly to Las Vegas to shoot some promos for Apple Bottom.

While in Vegas, Yomi and I had an important and pivotal conversation. He asked me what I wanted to do with my life and that if I needed help buying equipment, he would help me. This was the first time someone really believed I had the potential to do something big. Immediately after that he referred me to his friend. His friend then hired me to shoot the Nelly and Bow Wow basketball tour. Yomi became my main client and a close friend.

After a year I was back at his house, shooting another video with him and his children. That night I drove back to the city and I stopped by my friend's studio. While sitting in my friend's studio, I heard my car alarm go off. I got up and walked out the door to my car. I didn't see anything at first, but seconds later I noticed that my lights were blinking, and the car alarm went off again. I looked to my left and saw two guys down the street hopping into another car with all my camera equipment. These guys had busted my window and taken everything but my camera. I did not have much money at the time other than the money I earned from my videos, which I would invest back into my equipment.

Fortunately, a couple days after that I had a gig shooting an eye candy model contest at a nearby club. When I got to the club, my little brother was inside with his friends celebrating his birthday. Before the night was over, he had an issue with a bouncer who pulled him outside the club. I noticed what happened immediately afterward. I went out with him to put a stop to it, and by this time the police showed up and intervened while he spoke with my brother. Things escalated and the cops decided to lock him up. While they were putting him in handcuffs, I noticed my little sister and my brother's girlfriend were standing nearby. I walked over to pull the two girls away and as I extended my hands, one of the cops turned and hit me in the face. When he hit me, I automatically hit him back. Right after that, about five cops jumped on top of me on the ground. They hit me and blood was everywhere.

I don't remember everything, but I do know my mom came out and I heard her talking to the cops. They put my brother in the paddy wagon and then took the handcuffs off me. The cop let me go and told her that I didn't do anything; I was just at the wrong place at the wrong time. As I was walking away, I leaned on the gate because I couldn't see. I heard another cop walk over and asked why he let me go. Then he told him since they put their hands on me, they had to lock me up. The cops came and got me and took me back to the paddy wagon. My brother and I were taken down to the precinct and locked up. I asked to be taken to the hospital because I had a lot of blood on me and I didn't want the cops wiping it off.

Once I got to the hospital, the doctor came in and told them I had a fractured nose. The cop that was in the room with me at the time knew me from playing in the police basketball league. He tried to apologize for what had happened. I thanked him for giving me a criminal record and messing up my life more than it already was.

After I got out of the hospital, I was locked up for 48 hours. This was my first time ever being in jail. I could not believe that I was in jail. I could not believe the way I had been treated and I never wanted to feel this way again.

After I got out of jail, I looked at my bank account and realized I didn't have enough money to do anything other than pay my rent and get food. I was suspended from my job until they could find out if I had done anything. Everything seemed to have fallen apart again. I went from jail to the steak restaurant that was next to my apartment. I promised myself that I would never be in this position again. After eating the steak and drinking red wine, I went into my apartment and sat in the dark. All I could think about was what would my grandma have me do, and it came to me. For the next two weeks I was in my apartment praying. I didn't have any money and I had lost my camera. I was disappointed because I thought I had finally gotten my stuff together. While praying, Sunni crossed my mind, so I looked at my phone and I still had his number.

I called him and asked him if he could help me get a job as a Production Assistant (PA). I even offered to pay my way to Chicago. He told me that I would have to get a job in my city for things to work out. I told him there was no film industry in St. Louis and that I would call him again. Sunni called back and told me to call another lady who was in my city and ask her. It just so happened when I called the lady, she was hiring Production Assistants for BET Sunday Best, a gospel show. BET was coming to St. Louis for one week to do the travel gospel show. She hired me as a PA. Throughout that week I worked hard. I networked whenever I could. By the end of week, I had an offer to stay and work for two more days shipping everything back to Atlanta.

The production manager, Chazz, walked over and invited me to come down to Atlanta to the station. He told me if I did not have a place to stay, I could stay with him. During the week that the BET crew was in town, I spent a lot of time hanging out with the guys after work. I got to know them well in a short amount of time. I even spent time with the boss lady. At the time I did not know anyone's position, I was genuinely being myself, fortunately she and I clicked well. Once BET left town, I went back to work at the juvenile detention center. Although I continued to work at the detention center, I anxiously waited on a call back from Chazz. I received the call back a month later. One day while sitting in my apartment I texted him and asked if he had any information when the show would start. He responded that he thought he said sent a text message and that my start date was the coming weekend. I could not believe it. I picked up the phone to call him to make sure that I had read the text right.

After he confirmed, I began packing my things from my apartment. The next day I went to work and told them that this would be my last week. The superintendent asked me if I wanted to take a leave of absence just in case it didn't work out. I told him that not working out wasn't a choice. I called a friend of mine who was the dean of students at the college I went to and asked if he could help me get a flight down to Atlanta. He had his wife purchase my flight and I gave my apartment to a family member and left town.

I arrived in Atlanta and for 30 days I worked as a PA on BET Sunday Best. After 30 days it was tough for me to go back to St. Louis. I returned home and realized that I had spent all the money I had made. I wanted to make TV my full-time job. While I was waiting, I received calls from multiple people who worked on the project. I was shocked every time I received a call. I did not think these people had paid attention to me as much as they had. They kept me encouraged. After being home for 30 days, another PA named Darnell, who I would later become friends with, invited me to work on a project in Detroit. It was only for a week. He let me know that he was planning to move back to Atlanta too. So, I went back home, jumped in my truck, and drove to Atlanta with a hundred dollars in my pocket. I ran out of money by the time I got to Chattanooga, Tennessee. I had a cousin who lived in Atlanta, I called him, and he sent me money to make it the rest of the way. I made it back to the guy's house who hired me for my first PA job in Atlanta.

Here I was, a 29-year-old man who knew nothing about TV. I was down in the ATL where it seemed like everybody had it together. I was in a daze; it was so unreal to me. This was the second time in my life I felt like I was doing something people did not expect of me; going to college was the first. I had never imagined working in TV, and it was a big deal to me. Because I worked as a PA in St. Louis, I knew that was not where I wanted to stay. I did not know the hierarchy yet, but I knew that I wanted to move up. I was too old to be getting lunch orders for people. Normally as a PA your job is to do what you are told, do it well, and stay in your lane. I sort of knew that, but I did not always adhere to it. As a PA I saw an opportunity that could change my life, so I did what I knew best: I made myself visible to everyone by doing more than I was asked to do, and I asked a lot of questions. Before moving to Atlanta and working at BET, I had never seen so many successful Blacks that had jobs I considered cool. I never wanted the production of that season to end. By the time it was over, everyone was treating me like family. I couldn't believe it; it was a dream come true. This was where I landed after running around St. Louis with a camera shooting club videos and promos, not what I consider major. I knew now that I was a part of making a major TV show. I quickly settled into my new life. I knew that there were a lot of people who came to this city to do what I was doing. I even found out that some had gone to school to be in this business and that intimidated me a bit, but I was willing to work as hard as I had to make this something with longevity. All I had was my name and my work. The most impressive part to me, was that everyone was Black, polite, and helpful.

One day I walked into the wrong room looking for trash to pick up, and the showrunner, Marilyn Gill, was sitting in a meeting with her team. She saw me walk in, before I could step out, she invited me to come and sit in on the meeting. I sat there nervously because this was something I had seen on TV and I knew I was out of place.

I listened as they discussed the creative plans for the week. They got to a point where the room was voting on an idea. After hearing everyone else, she turned and asked what I thought. I gave my opinion, and when I left the meeting I went straight to the restroom and thanked God. I knew in my heart that I was where I was supposed to be.

I day-played some shows and worked on others so that I could make sure I had income. Day play means that you only work that day, unless asked to return for another day's work. I also had the opportunity to work at Tyler Perry Studios on three different productions. That was a big deal for me. Another big opportunity came for me when I became a day player on a Bravo show called "The Kandi Factory," starring Kandi from the Housewives of Atlanta, I met a lady by the name of Joye Chin. Joye was the executive in charge of Housewives of Atlanta, at the time I did not know what that meant, and I was not familiar with the show Housewives of Atlanta. One day I got a call from Joye and the production manager Angel Johnson. They talked to me, on the phone, for about an hour. I was in the middle of an interview, but I did not know it until the end. My first big show was working on NeNe Leakes' Wedding Special. After working on that,

I was offered a field coordinator position on Real Housewives of Atlanta. It was not an easy job; it was a challenging show to shoot. I embraced it, worked hard, and learned.

Fast forward, Marilyn would become like a mom to me. In 2014 she assigned me my first associate producer job. Such a surreal moment. I called my mom and told her to continue to pray because I was going to be successful and help the family like I always wanted to do. My mom did not know what a producer was, but she was proud to hear I was working in television.

I told a few people back home when it happened, but it didn't register until they saw my name on TV. I had finally beat the odds: the fatherless, homeless high school dropout was now a TV producer! After being an associate producer on season 7 of BET Sunday Best, I would become an associate producer on Real Housewives of Atlanta (RHOA) season 7. I continued and worked my way up in 4½ years from PA to executive producer. My journey as a producer required me to adjust to a new profession and life. Most of the guys I identified with were camera guys and camera assistants. Most of the producers were either women, White, or gay guys. I was told that I would never have the opportunity to be a producer if I was not gay. My work ethic went into overdrive. I am that person. When told I cannot do something it inspires me to try harder. One thing I learned quickly is that in this business you must be able to talk to people from all walks of life. That was not a problem for me, I moved around so much growing up, I came across a lot of people. It was one thing that I learned while trying to survive: relationships are just as important as money. So many things about producing I learned on the fly. If there was something I did not know how to do I would stay up nightly working on those things at home until I figured it out. One thing that worked well for me was making the most of my relationship with the cast members of the show. My approach was to always understand that people are real, and that if you stay true to yourself, people appreciate that more. Honestly, it is a blessing to have a career where I can be my authentic self with people.

I worried. I was afraid that I was not going to make anything of myself. I worked hard and encountered many setbacks. However, I finally made a career choice which led me to a career in television. It has been an amazing transition; my circumstances began changing right in front of my eyes. Small things changed, like going to the club and the bouncers and promoters making sure I was able to walk in without a problem, to getting calls to shoot video at private places when celebrities came to town. When it first started happening, it was a big deal to me. It wasn't long before that happened, I only saw these celebrities, as well as other well-known people in the industry, from a distance. They were the popular people in the city. It was a sign of progress, and it was the motivation I needed to continue pushing forward. My excitement seemed like bragging to the people that were close to me. I was on a level where all the local rappers, promoters, club owners, and public figures were important to me. These were the people I needed to know, and it was happening. My plan was taking off. As I made more progress, I got a real sense of who was who and where I needed to focus my attention. Some of the people I thought I needed to know needed my help to keep their image relevant. Knowing this, made me more confident. I was able to leverage my knowledge and talent to add value to others while doing something I loved. As I became well-known in the city, my initial plan required change. My initial plan became a short-sighted goal. I aimed low and hit my mark. I could have stayed home and got caught up in the allure of partying and being seen with the who's who. I reevaluated, as well as redefined what success meant to me. There are levels of success, and I knew I wanted a higher quality of life. I acknowledged that what I was doing was not lucrative enough or sustainable enough for me to achieve my new definition of success.

I feel like I went from failure to possibility, to success. How did I get here? I hope I'm doing things right. Why me? It's really working. I can do this by making plans and setting goals to achieve in the business. These were some of the thoughts that haunted me at times but challenged me to develop a solid plan where failure was no longer an option. It took some time to shake off the thoughts and beliefs I carried around. Moving to Atlanta was a breath of fresh air. It allowed me to look at life through a different lens, one that I always knew existed, the lens of tangible hope. I had an opportunity in my hands. It forced me to fully expose myself. If I wanted to succeed, I had to let out that hopeful kid I've always had inside of me. I started to visualize myself being successful. It wasn't hard to do when I was waking up every morning and going to work on a TV set. There was nothing I noticed on my path that signaled I was going to be a professional creative with the executive title behind my name. I was happy to have a chance to fully apply myself. The first part of my life was riddled with broken promises and scams. Here, in Atlanta, I had to trust the word of those around me; if I did not, I was going to end up back in St. Louis.

Looking back, I feel like things began working for me because I had begun to act as if I deserved it. I did a lot of local work in St. Louis. I was working at the juvenile detention center in the daytime and videoing in the club late at night. I was making only $800 dollars every two weeks, so my pockets were jammed, but I would still find a way to use some of my paycheck to buy equipment. As long as the bills were paid, I bought what I needed. It took over a year before I made a reasonable profit from my work. I knew I was doing something right when Yomi Martin, I mentioned him earlier, invited me to an upscale restaurant in one of the nicer suburbs in St. Louis. I sat down to eat with one of the owners of Apple Bottom Jeans, I was beginning a new journey. Once I got there, I walked over to the bar and sat down. He acknowledged me, but we didn't speak until after the food was ordered and on the table. He pointed out that this was my first lesson from him: you break bread before talking business. Then he did something I'll never forget. He asked me why I seemed nervous. Before I could speak, he told me that there should never be anyone I encountered where I felt I was not good enough to be in their presence. This struck a chord with me. I used to tell the kids at the juvenile detention center the same thing Yomi said to me that night., I was nervous because all I did was grab a camera from school one day and decided that I was going to start working for myself. Now here I was in front of a young rich guy who was genuinely embracing me like a brother! My mind was all over the place with nervous excitement. I had a not-so-clear vision in my head of doing something major, and I was seeing bits and pieces as it began to materialize. Still, I did not have an idea of how things would turn out, I was happy to be in acquaintance with a bro.

Leaving my family and my familiar surroundings forced me to increase my faith in God. A big part of me felt like I loved the things I was experiencing. Often, I found myself being around others when they were having major issues and before I'd part ways with them, it seems they would find a solution. I'm sure it sounds crazy, but because of those experiences I feel like part of my purpose is to be a shoulder and a beacon of light to whomever God puts in my presence.

I am still trying to understand my life. I experienced many things that helped mold and shape me as a person. Some good, some bad. I do not know which ones had the most impact. Some of the bad things helped open my eyes to see what I needed to do. I used to think to get anything good in life, you had to go through a lot of bad things. This was not true. I learned as I matured that sometimes bad things, tragic things, even horrible things happened to good people with a comfortable life. One day I was talking to a guy named George Brooks who told me as a Black man he grew up in a good family. Overall, things were good in his life, this guy was overly successful. I realized there are many ways to live life, and there is not one route to success. I have always heard that hard work and focus was the way to succeed. What amazed me the most is that although George did not grow up the way that I did, we had a compatible understanding of life. He did not adopt the belief that things have to be bad before they get good. It was such a relief to me. In that moment I knew that I had the ability to break the habit of negative thinking and anticipating a crisis. Although I was making progress in my life, I was still expecting something bad to come first before anything good could happen.

I understood my feelings. I knew that it was up to me to do the work to move from negativity to positivity, it had to begin in me. I had to pivot. For a long time, I was caught up in what I thought people should be thinking about me. I was concerned about why they weren't doing the things I thought they should. Instead, I should have been focusing on what I was going to do and reclaim control of my life.

My cousin John-John (John Shawler), worked in the music industry, came to me one day while I was staying with his mother. We were talking and I was telling him everything that I wanted to do. He stopped me mid-sentence and told me how he was tired of hearing how people wanted to do things, but they don't do them. He told me to just go out and try. "Just do it," he said. "A man has more control over his life than anything else." He then told me if I made progress that he would help me. That is another conversation that I never forgot. Although I may have heard it in school, this time I listened to someone who I knew had done something major. John-John went to Howard University, but left school to be a drummer for the singer Roberta Flack. He told me, before going to college, that he would go to the House of Blues, sit in the back, and watch the bands loading equipment. One day he asked if they needed any help. The guy let him help load and unload the equipment, which led to building a life-changing relationship. He found an entryway into the world of music, where he wanted to work.

His example was simple and painted a clear picture for me. I wanted to go to college and play basketball. His words motivated me and became the reason why I went to the local schools in Chicago. His words gave me the courage needed to walk into those gyms and into those practices. I was brave enough to talk to the coaches to get on the team. Using that as my primary incentive, I learned that being bold, working hard, and being consistent opened many doors for me. I took risks, I had nothing to lose. Often, we do not make moves because of how we see ourselves.

Even at times when I questioned God, there was something spiritual happening in my life. I always looked for signs or listened to people to hear if they said anything that sparked something inside me. I can honestly say along the way God has put a special person in each one of my circumstances to help me get through. Even the people who did horrible shit to me helped me gain the strength that I needed to continue pushing through hard times.

My journey taught me how to be understanding and forgiving. I have forgiven people who were close to me. It was easy to forgive when I started looking at things from more than one perspective. Thinking about my mother, I wanted things to be a certain way with her, but I had to accept that she did the best that she could with me. My mother was strong and to this day a lot of things that she told me I hold on to. She gives the best advice because she has a lot of life experience. Had I not understood that she too was a victim of circumstances and not realized that she may have not gotten all she wanted in life, I may have held a grudge against her, and I think I would have missed out on many positive experiences. Now I know that part of my frustration with her was because I was also frustrated with myself. I wanted to help her, but the timing was so bad. I wasn't old enough to do anything effective. I ran away from home thinking I would make something major happen and come back, but my journey became turbulent and I got caught up in day-to-day survival.

For a long time, I did a lot of living without intentional planning. I did reactive planning. It was far too often, I was just floating around, day to day surviving. That is a straight path of failure. Regardless of the ambition you claim to have, if you don't have a plan then you are more likely to end up where someone else wants you to be versus where you want to be. It really wasn't until I went to LA that I started learning that I can make plans and I can make things happen.

CHAPTER TWELVE
Roads Traveled

WHEN YOU LOSE faith in almost everything and everyone, you begin to question your existence. Any shred of confidence I had, began to slowly diminish. I began to dissect and question everything around me. It is a dark space to be in, but in a weird way it is a blessing in disguise. I say this because for some of us when we are in dark places, that's when everything matters the most. I know it can have the opposite effect on people and make them give up. It was in the dark recesses of my mind that I started to let go of my ego and pride. I had to acknowledge my shortcomings, embrace them, and make moves with the intent to find a solution. Sometimes I felt like I looked stupid to others, I had to let that go, and sometimes I lived as a loner. I remember when I was at rock bottom, I was like, "Fuck it, no one is coming to save me". I started demanding better. I stopped smoking, I cut back on hanging with friends, and I started praying more. I had tried everything else. Hitting rock bottom pretty much sent me running to God. I wanted a life change so bad that although the pastor told me to wait on God, I was too impatient, so I asked God to be patient with me. I approached every move I made with all the seriousness I could muster up. Progress was being made but I still wasn't in a place where I was consciously believing, I was only believing at the time because I had no option and was too afraid to see what was on the other side of my going back in that dark space. There was a turning point. I recall starting to believe in living after seeing that the moves I made were rendering positive results. That was a different mental space for me. I had a different type of pride in those moments. It was not the pride I spoke with when defending myself from someone's criticism, it was that sense of self pride you get when people acknowledge your accomplishments. This type of thing may seem simple to the average person in a safe and supportive environment. In the "hood," the simple things are not free. You must earn smiles and compliments that aren't backhanded, you must earn self-confidence. It is a gift when you hear someone other than the girls you are sleeping with genuinely proclaim, they love you for just being you. Holidays may seem great on TV, but in some households, they do more damage than good. Many people do not understand the mindset of Black boys who grow to be men in this type of environment. We are often silent, crying on the inside but the turnup king when we are with our friends. Our belief systems usually only work in the hood, business, or in cutthroat situations. The basis of our belief system is a survivor's mindset. That is a curse. Living in a survival state of mind keeps you on edge and distrusting of people, as well as anything else outside of your control. The saddest thing about that to me is witnessing many guys like me living and dying without the opportunity to experience pure love, a beautiful and healthy environment, the feelings of hope and faith without having to usher it in through pain. They say that you can't miss what you never had, that's not true. During my days of disbelief, my eyes were the most open they'd ever been. I was aware of the gated communities, clean school, vivid grocery store that sat on clean streets, and anything else that was not in the "hood." Seeing those things always reminded me that I was part of a world that no one cared to see. Imagine being a teenager walking around with that in the back of your head every minute of the day. Pain is good when it hurts so bad that you go numb and start working on a plan. Pain is not good when it hurts so bad that you start to self-destruct.

There are groups of young Black kids, boys and girls, walking around trying to find their way. Staring at the world through project window screens and wishing on a star. It baffles me how people see the environment we come out of but still put the same expectations on us that they expect from someone who has been blessed with a plethora of resources. Being poor and black in America is riddled with challenges. Then on the flip side, punishment comes from the heaviest of hands. I know this may seem like an excuse to some, but I hope that people can look past that and deal with us with empathy--we are worth fighting for! As the poet Gil Scott-Heron wrote in the song A Sign of the Ages, "The world's full of children who grew up too fast." That is all too true in the poor Black neighborhoods in America. Children are entitled to experience a childhood free of adult circumstances, pressure, and worry.

I have always empathized with people I grew up with. I was able to reason on an adult level and I recognized when their perception of life would be detrimental. In our neighborhood you could be killed or beaten up by the cops for stealing food or playing around too much like young people do. For young White guys who lived in a nice community, they would not be treated that way for the same actions and behaviors. I knew that at a young age. Hence, my empathy toward my friends. I knew that some of my friends lacked awareness of the world we were living in, some of their reality was skewed simply because we were all young. Unfortunately, many would find out the hard way once their interaction with the cops began. I tried to have conversations with my peers, most were not ready to hear, care or even try to understand that we all were operating at a social-economic deficit. I made many mistakes, but I think what made a difference in my life was my ability to take positive risks. In all walks of life, the old saying, that you can lead a horse to water, but you can't make them drink, is true. On the other hand, that same saying has always been hard for me to accept. I knew then and still know now, that by not drinking the water we all are lost in this environment that was planned from the heart of those who hate us. It was hell for me, and I consider myself in-tuned with reality, so I empathize with the hardships of the neglected.

I always felt it was such an unfair world for us as Black men. Traumatized and stripped of our masculinity, we have access to limited outlets to express our pain. We often go on like nothing never happened, while trying to assert our right to be men and retain our masculinity. All the while the people who study our communities can guess our behavioral responses to a given situation before we can. We are often around people who are victims of the bullshit too, and they haven't noticed the negative effects it has on their lives. They even pass on detrimental belief systems and behaviors to us, which we fully embrace and find rational as to why it makes sense. Many of us know people who say, "This is the way GOD made me," when really that is not the truth. It is far too often an excuse to behave recklessly, without accountability. Some of us do not find out who we are supposed to be until we make a shitload of mistakes. The change that comes with our awareness and acknowledgement of those mistakes can be transformational. Once we settle for whatever level of life we fought our way to, our vision clears, and we begin to understand that we can do more and become a better version of our better selves. More than likely, coming from a deficient environment we may realize that the level we strove for was a lower level than it should be. Many of us are traumatized and our responses are emotional, once again reflective of a sub-standard environment focused on survival. We do our most important thinking, trapped in a reactive emotional state. We make emotional decisions that lead to permanent outcomes that not only are based on logic but are just as precarious as the emotions they were based on at the time. Moreover, what is worse than emotional uneducated thinking? We are making life decisions with low-level thinking. All the while the emotions we carry as a disenfranchised people sometimes stem from misinterpretation, and faulty perceptions. As a young kid I began to see this very thing manifest in my life. I have been a part of several traumatic situations and woke up the next morning each time being told to shake it off. The funny thing about that is in the real world you really must learn to shake shit off. Resiliency can be the defining factor in life. However, it is not acceptable to shake shit off when it becomes the remedy for your constant bad decision-making. Looking at my life, I realized that I did a lot of shaking it off while I was under the supervision of others and partly when I became my own man. Although I am proud of the man I am today, I know for sure I would be an even better man if I addressed my issues and got support earlier in the game.

As the years go by, I have these random moments where I look at my family and am amazed at all the unexpected things, I didn't imagine us doing when I was a kid. To see my older brother married, my younger brother traveling, having his own business and teaching, and just knowing that my daughter will be in college soon is a mind-blowing blessing. All these things are simple and should have been expected, but I believe that as a child and teenager I experienced so much disappointment and failure that I mentally went into a shell and eventually my complete focus was on how to get out of the situations I was in, as well as how to avoid falling back or entering new challenges.

I wasn't living, I was surviving; I did not have peace of mind. Let me say it again, I was not living, I was surviving in a state of constant fear. For at least a year or two, I was scared as shit. I did not know what steps to take to better my life and I did not have anyone I trusted to guide me. I was still a young boy being treated like a man. I never experienced a moment without worry. No peace, overwhelming stress, and constant insecurities, I dealt with them all alone, staying silent except during the moments in my life where I felt God had sent an individual to give me temporary relief. Those people provided just enough normalcy that I was able to walk away from them feeling like I was no longer alone in the world. Those infrequent times reinforced my belief that all I had to do was keep trying and believing.

Those people who offered me mental and physical rest, were a reminder that someone was always watching, and at the time that was my desire, someone to watch, someone to notice me. I felt invisible and alone growing up, it felt good and reassuring that I mattered when someone noticed me. If I saw someone paying attention, that helped; I let my crazy brain do the rest of the work. I would plant a seed in my own head, telling myself that person cared and loved me, even if they did not tell me. Of course, I knew it was not real, but I needed to tell myself that I must keep going.

In my case, "I found strength in make-believe love." Now that only worked when I was in control of the narrative and the interactions with the person was limited. In my relationships, I could not bring myself to be comfortable with fake love. I cared too much about the other person to allow them to be unhappy dealing with me, so I would pretty much shut down until they left me. My dysfunctional coping skills always expected them to leave anyway. I moved around so much that having consistent friends and consistent places to live was not my normal way of living. Eventually it was difficult to attach myself to anyone or expect people to stay around long.

There was a point in time where I did give all of myself to someone: the most common situation –my first love. In the beginning she was a lifesaver. I did not experience love or feel important until I met her. I was 16, so after 16 years of feeling like I didn't matter, I met an extremely beautiful girl who told me she loved me, hugged, and kissed me—I mean, I could not get enough, and she could do no wrong. I used to love when she wore pink and white. She was my angel, but the life I always knew was still with me. My love affair with her ended in more pain and heartbreak than I have ever experienced. To this day I still feel that love hurt me more than helped me. Don't get me wrong; I had a few significant people come into my life, love me and make a difference, but unfortunately being human, the love I want the most is that of a companion, and that is the love I struggled to find peace with.

I learned what not to do watching the moves other people made and listening. To get information, wisdom, and advice, I used to go to the old head bar and talk to the mailmen and drunks, tell them about my problems, but I always presented my problems as if they were someone else's. I'm fond of old folks and their wisdom. When I was on my own roaming the streets, one of my favorite pastimes was talking to the old heads. The crackheads, drunks, mailmen, whoever was on the strip, I talked to them all. I figured any Black man that made it to be as old as they did have some type of information I could use. Most of the guys I talked to were unsuccessful and struggling; their focus was staying alive and trying to get through the day. I looked at them as a collective of bad decisions, and I think anyone who's made a shitload of mistakes has some knowledge.

It worked for me, I was good at putting two and two together and learning what to do by outcome. I always had an old head friend that would get me in the local hole in the wall. Once in there, I'd have a few drinks and do some ear hustling. I loved hearing the stories these guys would tell. I would then tell them about a problem a friend of mine was having. Of course, I was talking about myself. I think they knew but never called me out on it. After one person would give me their point of view, I found a way to get another point of view from someone different.

The best advice I got was from an older off-duty mailman. My guy had on a Dobb, pinky ring and a three-quarter mink coat. His advice was priceless. He told me to remember that I will attract the energy I put out. Always expect that at some point what I do will make its way back around. I took that to heart; it was what I needed to hear. After I talked to these old guys, I would go where I stayed that night and replay what they said over and over in my mind. Some of the guys' advice made me feel like I was better off without a father, especially if he was anything like them. I could tell that some of them felt like they were redeeming themselves by giving me heartfelt advice. One thing for sure: they all told me I had a good brain, and I was going to make it.

Although I took their advice, it was hard to believe I was going to survive past 21. I could not see a way out of my struggle. The good thing is my method of sourcing those guys' opinions worked; it helped me gain a better mindset when it came to my perspective on how life was supposed to be. I learned from the old heads that no one owed me anything, and I had to figure this shit out 'cause life wouldn't ever be easy on a nigga. Also, I learned that all I had to do in any environment was to just be patient and listen to the talkers, then I'd be able to formulate a plan on how to maneuver. Honestly, I did feel like life owed me something for all the trouble I had been through and was going through at the time. They were all telling me that, so I didn't walk around with the expectation that a handout was coming. In our world a handout normally meant what you were getting wasn't any good or you ended up in debt with someone.

Understanding that no one owes me anything put things in perspective. It was clear to me that no one owed me their honesty. I knew that if I wanted something, I had to go after it ready to do the work. My faith could not solely be in people. I put my faith in God, my work, my work ethic, my allies, and my ability to continue to keep moving after being told no.

Moving like that has made the unexpected happen. I have gained respect from people that I know have doubted me. It feels good because the only thing I ever asked them for was an opportunity. Sadly, I didn't expect that would come; I just stayed ready for whenever the time came.

The world seems different when people you look up to, look up to you. Especially by the same people who looked down on you. As I began to progress in life, I started noticing that some of the people who I looked to for advice started asking me for advice. That was when I knew that I was headed in the right direction. Also, through conversations, I realized a lot of people had their minds made up about how my life was going to be. They figured since I had so many hard times, there was no way I was going to find a way out. It was such a shock to many, and I understood that, because I was shocked at myself. From the one that my strides didn't intimidate, I received many questions about where did I get the courage to try, what made me think I was good enough to hang around the people in my city who were known?

This was a clear indication that I was around a lot of people who had dreams. At times they made me feel like I had done something special. I did not feel like I had done something special; what was surprising to me was that I felt in my heart that life had more for me, and I was watching it materialize. It was a bit scary because all along I was taking advice from these people and applying it to my life, and it was working for me, and now I was hearing them tell me that they'd failed at their attempts to succeed at what they dreamed of. Now it was my turn to share my knowledge, but I was also concerned about who I was going to talk to now so that I could continue to make moves in this new arena. I had to understand that because they had questions for me didn't take anything away from them. What I had just experienced is the old saying, "The student becomes the teacher."

I was coming into myself. Deep down I always knew I'd be a voice that had valuable information for others. This helped build my self-esteem, and it made me believe even more that I deserved to be where I was headed.

One principle I will always keep is to be a giver. I feel Black men are treated like shit from the womb to the tomb, so we must have each other's back. My empathy is deep for us. There is no feeling like being a giver, so when it comes to anyone I see working hard, I do whatever I can within my power to help. Most Black men are not given anything, even when working hard and deserving. That is why I try to show support and love to my brothers.

I learned to reevaluate everything I have been taught. The reevaluation process has helped me better understand when to apply the appropriate knowledge to a problem. Our lives constantly change, but we use the same methods of action in changing situations. That can be detrimental. Approaching every situation with the same mindset will lead to failure before it leads to success. Acting off assumptions; assuming that the current circumstance is identical to the last, means if there is any new information to learn, you possibly have closed a window to learn. So, the desired outcome is not what the true outcome should be, that thing you don't really want to happen happens, the thing you are afraid of manifests. Just think if you approach a conflict with the idea of getting an update first, you may find out something that would turn everything around, which can lead to the positive more desired outcome.

One morning while in college, I ran into a friend and he was pissed. Instead of going to class, he was leaving school, yes dropping out. He wouldn't tell me much other than the fact that someone pushed him the wrong way. I strongly suggested that he get all the facts before he made a move. I assumed that he was probably mad at his chick, so I told him do not assume or respond to the situation emotionally. It ain't too many niggas around like us at this school, I said. I continued by reminding him that we been through the shits and we were trying to get right. Then we parted ways. A week later Kevin Powell, author of "The Black Male Handbook", spoke at our school. Mr. Powell held a guys' talk in the school auditorium, only a few of us showed up, mostly the fraternity guys. I was there, and my friend from the other day was there. I was surprised to see him because I had not seen him since our talk.

During the talk, Kevin told us that we need to let the people who have changed our lives or helped us, know that we appreciate it, sooner rather than later. My friend stood up and asked if he could talk. Next, he asked me to stand up and I did. He told me that my talk with him the other day had changed his life. He told me that he had been headed to the dorm to clean out his room and then he was going to the east side to kill someone, but after talking to me he took my suggestion and let the whole thing go.

Honestly, I teared up because I love my friends. I have lost very young and important guys in my life to stuff that should have never happened. He and I hugged, and we took our seats. We did not talk about that anymore. We left it there; the love was understood. He kept updating me on the good things that happened to him afterwards. What that did for me was powerful. I felt like I had saved two people's lives and kept families from hurting. Although I was comfortable talking to anyone on any level, this made me want to do more and pay more attention to the people I loved and cared about. Had my friend or I operated out of certain principles we were taught growing up in our environment, such as staying out of other people's business and not talking about your problems outside your house, there would have been more hurt, and pain added to our atmosphere.

One thing I always keep in mind when dealing with my people is that despite all the bullshit I went through, I must understand there is a good chance the other person had similar experiences or worse. It may not be the case, but it is, often. I remember how I felt during those experiences, and I saw what it did to my loved ones, and those negative experiences are not something I want to pass on. Furthermore, I joke a lot with people, hoping that the laughter of my energy in the room adds something bright to their day. I used to wonder why it is that we gravitate to all the hurtful things about ourselves, then we find a way to make it cool. Why do we glorify, in our music, being a side chick or selling drugs, or calling each other names?

I have always been a family guy and a lover of people. More importantly my brief experience with my aunt and uncle in Minneapolis helped me achieve a better understanding of how a home should operate. Seeing them work in business together and run a family, I understood the effect of good teamwork. They made an impact on me. They both were hard workers and good people. My uncle's politeness and attention toward me allowed me to see how it felt to be on the receiving end of someone's care. I interact with other people keeping in mind that they could be going through something and now I am in their life I need to make sure that I am doing the best I can to make the greatest, most positive, impact on them.

I know firsthand how that positive energy can be the beginning of someone being opened to change or it can change a person's life for the better. It is rare to get a consistent balance of positive influence and positive feedback in some of the places I've lived. In those types of environments some people need daily encouragement and when it is not available it is easy to hear the many negative voices inside your head and outside infiltrating your environment. I witnessed brilliant people become angry and ungrateful towards life, and rightfully so. The people they encountered in life taught them to focus more on their hardship then all the possibilities the world has to offer. I know this to be true. I was that way until I encountered the presence of the right people. I often remind myself of how dark I used to see things, and today I'm grateful for the change. I try to share insight about my mental transition with others as much as possible. Each time we recognize something is good in our life, it helps build our faith and ability to be appreciative.

When my aunt and uncle allowed me to move in, they did not have to; they were assuming the responsibility of me and my care, that clearly was not theirs to assume. That is how far having compassion for others can go. They helped me, they chose to bring me into their home and devoted time and resources to make things better for me. Unc would always tell me to treat people right. Although I failed at listening to my uncle at some important moments, I made the decisions I did at the time because I felt that I deserved what I wanted after all I'd been through. At that time, I needed a break from thinking like an adult. I wanted to be a kid, so I did kid things, which led me back to an adult responsibility. My aunt and uncle did not disrespect me; they made their point known, required that I handle my business, and they supported me if they could. Today that is my approach with my daughter and others. I am a people lover; I like to start relationships by treating people the way I want to be treated, and once I see that is not working, I deal with them accordingly.

As the old saying goes, "Experience enhances your character." It is true in my case. My time in Minneapolis gave me the grounding and stability I needed to continue pushing. Having a break in between the struggle was important. I needed to let things settle in; I needed to reassess my life. I remember hearing a speaker explain how people may experience a situation more clearly after they have gone through it versus being in the moment. If I recall correctly, I think he was saying that when in the moment, you can only see certain things, and you are focused on making decisions. Afterward you can break down and analyze it all beginning, middle, and end.

Some things I learned did not register until later. The lesson or message from the situation would manifest, and I would surprise myself sometimes making a smart decision. Those old lessons were brewing inside of me, waiting for an opportunity to show up. The skills you learn in your trials become a part of your instincts, paired with your intellect. I believe that makes some people extraordinary.

Life can be extremely difficult when you are coming from "the bottom" and you are the first to lay a firm foundation in your family. There are so many unknowns you need to prepare for. As a product of a poverty-stricken environment, access to a healthy, whole lifestyle is limited. People around you may get involved in helping to make a change, depending on their influential reach, they can only get you to a certain point before you have to do the wise thing and seek more efficient help. Knowledge is power in every sense of the word when you are trying to move up in the world. You need to have knowledge of people and the business you are pursuing. I learned that you must be careful who you talk to about your dreams. It can intimidate people, and there's a chance you may be purposely given misinformation.

During the time I moved around a lot, I visited St. Louis at least once every year. I spent a lot of time with my older brother and sister. They each provided support in their own way. My sister, Kim, was like a second mom. Anytime I needed her, she was there for me. There was always a space in her home when I needed to be there. Her support had its limitations because of some personal things she was experiencing, but I always knew that she had my back. Although she left home at 16, she was aware of some of the obstacles the family faced.

She did what she could with what she had. Raising five kids alone and opening her door to the family was a lot, but she never said no. Kim and I have had a close relationship since I was a kid.

My older brother and I built a close relationship once he got out of prison. We spent many days hanging out and discussing real life issues. Talking to him sometimes was like being in my own head. Our relationship flourished at a time in my life where I needed his advice. Hanging with these two was part of my healing process. Most of my life I did not have many opportunities to spend time with them; we were always dealing with our own situations. Listening to them talk about their childhood helped me to understand more about my family and who I am. It brought us all closer together. For someone like me, I thrive on family; that is where I look for my strength. If there is a situation in the family that has not been discussed or resolved, I find it hard not to address it so we can move forward as a family. I felt the difference between the time I was away from the family and when we were all together. I love spending time with family. Even today I make sure to check on my siblings. Like many other families, not everyone is always in a good place, but we are close and share undeniable love one to another.

In my life, there has been someone significant who stepped in and pushed me past my own understanding. I relate it to sports training in a way. Sometimes you may not always understand what the coach is telling you, but you do what you are told repeatedly. When it's game time, what you have been working on shows up on the court. You perform, people applaud, and you go to that person and say thank you. It becomes clear later.

At times I knew I had to be okay with being misunderstood. I began to have a bigger vision for myself, but it was something I could not explain to other people. It was difficult at the time dealing with the criticism and misunderstanding, but I knew once I figured it out it would all make sense. I have tough skin, and I finally got to a point where I stopped seeking validation for a dream that was mine. I lived through this experience, as many others have, and I feel it is my responsibility to share my journey with others as a source of inspiration. I want you to know that your dream is not too big. That feeling you have inside that you cannot explain is the fire of change waiting for you to unleash it on the world.

CHAPTER THIRTEEN
To the Younger Me

IF I CAN tell myself anything, I would tell myself not to take everything so personally. So, I share that with you, do not take things so personally. I would remind myself that everything is not about me, in fact I learned that most things were not about me. The results of someone's decision is the summation of many different factors. I would tell my younger self to slow down and not worry so much. The things that I see aren't always going to be that way. I would help myself understand that no matter what I want to accomplish, it takes time and there is a process. I wish that I could go back to the time when I had my daughter and say, "It's okay, Markus, to stay in school and take your education seriously." I would comfort myself by saying, being afraid that you are going to be like your parents is not the correct approach. I would tell myself, if you keep thinking of all the negative things you do not want instead of thinking about the positive things that you want to do you are going to create bad things because your perception has you act in a way that will render the warranted results. Everything happens for a reason and you must find a way to adjust. Don't take it to heart. This is what I would say to myself.

The life I live today is amazing, and I am getting paid to do something I love. I feel like I am living the childhood I never had. My career has taken me all over the world. I have friends and acquaintances in all types of industries all over the world. Because the entertainment business is big on relationships, I go out and mingle when I have time. Normally it's a really cool place. Sometimes I am invited to parties that are being hosted by notable public figures. Besides all the cool and interesting things, I have access to, there is a lot of work involved, so I only get to do these things when I have time or if I am not tired from a long day and I decide to get out and mingle.

I work at least 12-hour days, which is standard. When I first started producing, I learned that a great producer knows something about everything. It is an unspoken professional requirement. We encounter people from all walks of life. Many of them have different lifestyles. Being resourceful, outspoken, and a people person had been a few of the secrets to my success.

It is my job to deal with the talent, with whom so far, I've been able to build at least a respectful rapport. I have worked on many different styles of reality TV, so l define myself as a versatile producer.

As I moved up, my role changed. I went from being on a team of people who did all the running around and making things happen to being over that team and leading them to accomplish the overall vision. Most days we have a plan, but because it is reality television, we know that there is a great possibility that anything can happen, therefore my days are exciting and filled with the unknown; we adjust through the day.

CHAPTER FOURTEEN
Realizing My Purpose

WORKING IN TV helped me realize that my passion is other people. In my career, one of my primary job duties is to communicate with others. I talk to cast members, to my workers, and to the network. I interact with people from different walks of life every day. I love it; it gives me energy. In each show, the teams are different, and I start over each time getting to know my team. It is a growing process that I enjoy. In my experience, as a producer of reality TV, I am typically the only heterosexual Black male in my position on set. I never allow that fact to be an obstacle. It has sparked some great conversations with people from different walks of life.

Working in reality TV, requires an understanding of people. By understanding people, you cannot be judgmental. You start to realize that everybody is not the same. For me to be an effective producer, I open-up and gain an understanding of the lifestyles of the cast members. To some effect, I have the indulgence of the world so that I can tell the story with as much truth as possible. The other trick to it is establishing rapport. I have learned not to treat people in the business as the business; our relationship is most important. The people in my field allow me in their homes and their personal business. The worst thing that can happen is for them to feel like I do not care or that I am disrespectful of who they are as a person.

On my resume there are many projects: Bravo's Real Housewives of Atlanta. The Housewives franchise is big. It is an extremely popular show in the Black, middle-class, and gay community. Most of the producing teams are comprised of gays and women. As a heterosexual man it feels good to have these people as my counterpart to establish a great working relationship. Every day I go to work I am privileged to learn something new. Furthermore, I show people that a guy like me can thrive and be genuine in any environment with anyone. Because of my career I have traveled all over the world and indulged in different cultures. As a friend of mine would always say, I have a dream job. Looking back on how I grew up, I can see how everything I went through prepared me for what I am doing today. Growing up I was always around a lot of different people, stayed in different homes or hotels, and traveled to different cities. That was pretty much my life growing up. This is the same for my career: I'm going to show after show, city to city, working with different people.

I have learned even more so working in TV that a person will never stop making mistakes and that does not make them worthless. Everyone makes mistakes every day, but as a team we cover each other, and we work together to correct the issues as they arise. Now, that does not mean a person should not do everything in their power to be great. The teachable moments are good for the teacher and the student. My rule is to stay a student of life but always be ready to initiate a plan of my own when an opportunity presents itself. Creative thinking is highly valued in this field.

Also, my career in television has allowed me to see the fruits of my labor. I am a hard worker and I feel that I have been rewarded and recognized for the effort and the care that I put into every project. Because of this I wake up every morning and jump out the bed, ready to get to work. I know that I help create something that is changing the lives and minds of others. This is a great feeling. Depending on the show, the cast members live different levels of lives. I worked on projects where I could relate to the members of the cast because their lives were somewhat like mine. It has helped me heal. I was a person who thought that my life would not amount to anything. Yet, I found my way into the television industry, and now I work with people who are like me: creative, driven, dreamers! Your TV crew becomes like family members because you spend 16/17 hours a day together for 3-5 months. We also grow close to the cast members and their families. We are in their homes and businesses, often taking up their personal space. Their kids grow up around us.

CHAPTER FIFTEEN
Where I Am Now

MY FAMILY IS still adjusting to my career. The business of reality television remains new to some people. I think it would be easier to understand for everyone if I were a cast member on the show. I explain that I am behind the scenes, so they all take my word for it. Because of my career I have been able to help multiple family members when needed, mainly my nieces and nephews. My siblings have made it clear that they are proud of me. My success is proof of the strength that we all share, and I try to use the allure of what I do to motivate when I get a chance.

My dream is to eventually own and operate a successful production company. I want to be able to give opportunities to not only my family but some of the talented and creative people that I come across who are just looking for a break. I have ups and downs, that is always part of living. I educate myself as much as possible, things are forever changing. I do not want to be too far behind learning about new technology and techniques, especially in my industry.

CHAPTER SIXTEEN
My New Goals

NOW THAT I have learned the things I know; my dream is bigger. I will own a production company one day. I want to use my production company to offer opportunities to people I meet, and that I know would not typically be offered opportunities based on politics. Currently I am doing all I can to learn every facet of this business. I do not want to limit myself working primarily in reality TV. I enjoy it but I know that I must have a long-range plan beyond what I currently contribute to the industry. I know I can offer more, such as writing this book. It is one thing I always wanted to accomplish. I have written a short film and I want to direct movies. I know all these things take time, so I am constantly working. I do not put too much on my plate at one time because I know the time and effort that goes into making one thing successful. If I can make this one thing successful it will open doors for everything else, I want to do. Furthermore, timing is everything, so I am trying to keep my eyes open to beyond the horizon in front of me, to see ahead, and have a clear vision to execute my plans at the right time.

One of my biggest dreams is to help my family members. Relationships are very important when it comes to business. I continue to build relationships; I have a long way to go. Then again, the way my life is going next week will change my life in a great way. The important thing is to stay diligent. I constantly work to improve myself; how I dress, how I speak, how I carry myself. I look to do better and be better as a man. I'm at a place in life where every day must count. I have come too far to stop and become complacent. I want to see other people flourish, and I want to put myself in a position so that I can get help for my dream, which is to have the resources needed to invest in people. There is no greater investment than investing in people. The more I build up people, the more those people can help others. I do not limit myself when it comes to thoughts and ideas because I am a big dreamer. Sometimes I can dream so big that it becomes overwhelming. I know that I am going to accomplish the things I have in mind. Moreover, one of my primary goals is to inspire others regardless of their status in life to dream and find a way to work toward their dream. Regardless of how ridiculous that dream may seem. I once heard someone say that if your dreams do not scare you, you are not dreaming big enough. How scary are your dreams?

We live in a time where I witness people, who look like me, accomplish major feats. The examples I did not see as a kid I am seeing ten times and more now. I don't need anyone to step out of time; sometimes I just see the existence of somebody else's motivation. I am motivated when I see the success of Calle or Jay-Z, Tyler Perry, Serena Williams, Robert Smith, or guys like Arnold Donald and George Brooks, whom I have met personally. I have always visualized myself in a position to inspire people. I do things my way, so I may need some refining when it comes to my choice of words, but my heart is lacking nothing when it comes to how much I care to see us all live the best lives.

I know I did not go through the things I did for nothing. Every small accomplishment I have had was done the opposite of what I was told was the correct way, but that let me know that it's an injustice to self when I don't try to do a thing because I don't have everything I need to start. My whole life is filled with unexpected situations I had to overcome. They say you repeat things in your life until you learn how to deal with them. I'm sure that I was supposed to learn to trust God and trust myself. Also, I had to learn patience. Once I got a hold of those things I started to thrive. Yes, my childhood was turbulent, but anything past the age of 15 I take full responsibility for. All the good and bad was my doing.

I survived because I was determined. I had the will to do so even when I was not conscious of it. I adapted to my environments and adjusted when needed. I kept in mind that if God did not hear me, he heard the prayers of my grandmother. That piece of faith was a part of my strength. The world is hard, but resilience evens the playing field. We become resilient when we believe we are capable of so much more than our elders would have us believe. As I stated earlier about not having anyone before me who laid the foundation, I know it is my job as a man in my family to set an example. Just as I am inspired by the people and things I see; it is the same for others. When I talk with my daughter, nieces, and nephews, I can see where their thinking lies. Each of them has spoken of being confused about what they want to do with their lives. I let them know how normal that is and that they need to expose themselves to more things. Now, being older, I can guess some of the obstacles they may encounter, and I do my best to try and open their eyes to those possibilities. It is not to incite fear but to teach them how there are some moments you just need to jump off the porch and there are moments where they need to be calculated. I do my part when I provide them with guidance and insight about the world. They will go on their own journeys, but they do not have to walk alone and blind.

Family legacy is important. It is something that I dream of starting and building for my family. Out of all the things I plan to do, being a family man is the most important. I find my greatest joy spending time with family. The level of success I wish to achieve is mainly because of the vision I have for my family, specifically my mother, daughter, nieces, and nephews. Where we are today, it is going to take the pursuit of financial freedom to get the ball rolling, paired with a new way of thinking about life. It is a huge undertaking; it is hard to get people to miss what they have never had. There are many things I have been able to experience that I believe will elevate the culture of my family. They are ambitious big dreamers, but the one thing I notice is that they all have not been exposed to many of the beautiful things in life.

Living in a beautiful home in an amazing neighborhood, international trips, and trips to a cabin does something to a person's spirit. It's such a great feeling to me and I want to share that with them. Some of them have brilliant minds, but they lack access to the level of education that will push them to their highest capability of intellectual thinking. Their reach is limited when it comes to building the proper relationships that are conducive to the life they deserve. As a man in the family, I am always concerned about the effects politics will have on them. Especially my nephews. I believe that every Black family should have it in their plans to become land, business, or homeowners as soon as possible. Each person should have something that they can leave behind for the next generation or something they can help each other with.

So far, my life has been an overwhelmingly eventful journey full of highs and lows. I've made strides in my life I deemed impossible. My level of growth has exceeded the expectations of many, and it has confirmed that unknown feeling that I felt inside. I'm so far from the boy I used to be, but I remain the same in spirit. My spirit is what carried me when I was living in a constant state of confusion. I have grown to a place where I feel that there's no environment or person that I cannot find a way to connect with and understand, even if I don't agree with who they are as a person. We must always keep in mind that as human beings we have so much more in common than we like to admit. Everyone has a different road and timing when they make it to the point of enlightenment. That is why it is important to share our stories with one another. Sometimes a person's form of strength comes from a stranger. I have learned many things from kindhearted strangers. Everyone is a stranger until you make them a friend.

Throughout my journey I have been solution-oriented and adaptable to new ways of thinking. If the solution I implemented is not working I make changes. That can be humbling. Acknowledging that your choice was not the right choice can make you feel like a failure. However, I quickly recognized the need to readily incorporate a new plan as needed. Remember earlier I said that one thing I would have told my younger self was to not take things personally. This is true when making decisions in your life. Why internalize a mistake? That is what I saw happening around me growing up in the hood. Resiliency is the key. Sometimes mistakes can wear you down, there were times when I felt exhausted from bad choices. But I knew that the only way I was going to make it was to change my approach and part of that was through learning, observation, and taking calculated risks. Furthermore, I developed principles as an intricate part of my plan. Principles are guidelines on how to operate your life, but you must be flexible when it comes to life. As I encountered different situations in different cities, I recognized the way that I thought about things in St. Louis didn't necessarily work in certain situations when I lived in Chicago. This is not to say that there are not some things I can bring from one place and take to another; you must recognize when what you are doing is improper for the time and place. I cannot emphasize this point enough. It is critical to success! In my case, things did not change for me until I was able to pay attention to myself to see what was working and what was not. The more I learned about myself, the more confident I became. The more I paid attention to what worked versus what did not work for me, the more my life began to take the shape I longed for. Traveling and living in different houses was life's way of making me the spectacular human being I am today. Yes, I think I am spectacular. Yet another key to success, if you don't think you are spectacular, why should others think you are spectacular? The thing is this, you are spectacular.

No longer do I think in extremes. I understand the road to perfection is a path of progress. Progress allows you to see the picture more clearly. Step by step, is the way I achieved my goals. Looking at others and their past gives you a false sense of what you need to do to get where you are going. I took note, so that I would know what not to do. However, that too is limited thinking. I began to understand that I needed to develop a strategy with specific steps to override my limited thinking, otherwise I would continue a downward spiral.

Some people blame everyone but themselves. For a long time, I dwelt on every wrong that was done to me, and I did not feel at peace until I started noticing options that I overlooked. I realized that I have control. Running away from home was empowering. It was something I came up with as a solution to a problem and executed it. I was in a difficult situation, and I was tired of my environment. I was forced to feel and experience life that was beyond my childlike comprehension. I knew the reality of life and how choices and words matter. In my environment, with the other guys my age, it was common for everything to be a joke. When something was serious, it was covered up and numbed by getting high or drinking.

It is not that we did not care; many of us faced adult situations, but we lacked the experience and life skills to attack them properly and give ourselves the best outcome. After going through situation after situation and feeling like I do not have any control, eventually I was tempted to give up. This is true for many young Black people living in impoverished urban areas, especially if there lacks a support system. I take great value in those people around me today who chose to open their mouth and say something uplifting to me. I will forever be grateful for the kind words and acts of service from those around me. I proudly and generously pass on uplifting gestures; I know what it does for the spirit.

I know when I see God's love in people. All my life, God has been with me through it all, even when I didn't know. My life today is proof that God and his vessels are around us every day. Praying carried me through many days where I had no idea of what I was going to eat or where I was going to stay. Miraculously, many of those times, someone came through to help meet my basic needs. Now I think that having a strong belief that God heard me, I was not afraid to open my mouth and reach out for help. Having faith in God gave me the courage to do the things I thought needed to be done regardless of what others thought. Looking back, there were moments I know I aimed low and was impatient with God. Because of my worry, I felt I needed things to move immediately. Had I waited longer or believed like I should have, my results would have been better. You know, that's the thing about life. Faith often requires waiting.

The definition of living is learning to experience the ups and downs and continuing to push through. Notice that I said "learning" to experience ups and downs and push through. That is an acquired skill for many. Taking hits from life is exactly like a video game: it shows you the character's energy level after every hit. It gets lower and lower because being hit takes something out of you no matter who you are. Others bounce back at different times, but we all absorb the blow. I wish we all could see each other's energy. More lives would be saved before it is too late. Nowadays I consider myself an energy person, and I believe that I can feel the energy of the person I am communicating with. When I feel there is something off, I tend to genuinely inquire about it.

People are my purpose. I love people and I want to help people. Even though I'm aware that the color of my skin is an obstacle to some of the people I encounter, I still care about them and treat them accordingly.

There are times I miss my old neighborhood. When I get back to visit St. Louis, I always drive through north St. Louis and reminisce. It's bittersweet because I lost some important people in my childhood who I wish could be here to celebrate with me. Remembering them keeps me grounded and hungry for greater success. When I first heard someone tell me that I made it out of the hood, I felt a way about that. I think it is called survivor's guilt. For a while I felt bad that it was me and not them, then I realized that I was looking at things the wrong way. Those friends I left behind in my old neighborhood would want me to achieve even higher heights for them. I am proud of myself! I am now one of the people in my family who is a positive role model for the younger generation. One day I will be an ancestor. I want my story to be part of my daughter's, her children's, and her children's children's history of triumph. I stick as close as I can to my siblings, cousins, nieces, and nephews, always trying to offer sound advice and encouragement.

I thrive on the sight of beautiful things. I recently drove through Bel-Air for the first time, and by the time I got through the hills my energy was way up. I was completely inspired by what I saw. I took in the energy from the beauty of the landscape. It was the total opposite of the places I grew up in, and that's fine. Now I have another level of life to strive for. That keeps me alive and hopefully having a goal to reach. Every day I look for things that inspire, and I notice there is always something that serves as a source of inspiration. Back then I focused on negativity. It was all I focused on, until I became more self-aware. I am happy to say I no longer focus on negativity. I hope one day I can reach out, find guys and girls like me, and take them on international trips so they can see how big the world is and how different their lives can be.

Other than my need to get back to my daughter, I wanted to make something of myself for my mom. Watching her struggle, I recognized the sacrifices she made. She gave birth to me and did what she could to instill qualities of being a good human being. I remember talking to her one day. I sat and listened as she shared with me all the things she had done in her life. I was surprised; she explained time periods in her life that I had not considered. I used to hear her, and her friends talk, but most of what they would speak about around us was thugs from their childhood. During our talk this time, I noticed how she would describe the things she did while working and how her work ethic contributed to her getting promotions. Then she would stop speaking. I think she wanted to avoid talking about why things did not work out as she had hoped. She did not have to tell me it was because she was a single mother.

People who have successful careers spend a lot of time away from home. She could not afford to do that; we lived in places where it was not safe for her to leave us alone for long periods of time. Also, she had limited help. Throughout my life when I tell my mom how something good happened at work, she had a story to relate and words of encouragement for me to continue pushing. Listening to her, I started to see that no matter how old a person is, there will always be some level of dreamer in them. I could hear, in her voice, how proud of her accomplishments she was. She told the stories as if they had just happened. I would engage her even more to get details of her environment and the people around. I swear after a while I could feel us both visualizing the thing each of us spoke of. Her level of pride and enthusiasm about certain things reminded me of myself. Talking to Mom on the phone helped me make sense of why she constantly made a point to tell me to be a man. She wanted me to know how good it felt to succeed in something. That was an important thing she did for me. In her own way she found a way to keep me hopeful. When you're hopeful you walk through the world looking and expecting that something is possible and good is going to happen to you. Being hopeful helps me make better decisions at times. Because I believed that although I wasn't anywhere near where I wanted to be, I felt like success, through my hard yet committed work, was going to happen one day.

I asked my mom one day what her dream job was. She told me that she always wanted to be a writer. She told me stories of how she used to grab her wine, light a candle, and sit at her desk and write. As she talked, I started to remember as a kid seeing her write. I told her it was not too late, and she should start now. I even said if she wrote a short film, I would help get it shot. After our talk it made me realize that there was so much more to my mom then I had known. This woman had big dreams and that's where I got it from. She and I are alike when it comes to big ideas and the possibilities of life. It has taken me a while to know what was in me and how it affected my thoughts and actions. I made a promise to myself that somehow, I had to help her see that she could still succeed on other levels, even if she had to live vicariously through me.

The day I became a producer I called and told her. She got excited, and like always, she began telling me her story about being a locator in the army. I could see she was holding on to her achievements, but she wanted more. That day I said thank you to her. I thanked her for the things she said while we were in hard times. I thanked her for making me a responsible man and told her that my success was hers.

It took a few years before I could celebrate with her. I flew her to Atlanta, and some friends came too. I took them out to a party, and they came on set during a shoot of RHOA. She had never seen me work before. I could feel her watching me. I waited for a while and when I turned around, the look on her face was priceless. It was like she had witnessed a miracle. She told me her prayer had been answered. I told her mine had been answered too. I made my mom proud; after all we had been through, I needed that. I knew she loved me, but I needed her to see what I was able to accomplish with little public education—another thing we had in common.

Being able to show my daughter and mom that I made something of myself gives me a sense of pride. I am not where I want to be, but I am also not a deadbeat dad or bum son.

Bad situations can turn into blessings. My struggles made me strong. I had to dig into myself and prove to myself that I could do the impossible, and every time I made a stride, I became stronger. Now it seems to me that the way my life went I had many areas of growth that were needed. The fear I had as a kid was different than the fear I had as a father and boyfriend. Those two things required me to take on different duties and approach the world in a way that aided those needs. My negative perception of life gave me a chance to go through the process of change and see for myself how powerful a changed mind can be. Also, as I transitioned from negative to positive, I started to experience life from varying perspectives thus giving me a sense of being well-rounded. I can have intellectual real-life conversations with people of all ages, colors, and creeds. Because of my love of knowledge and my need to better myself, I became a student of life. I searched for my better days like a pirate at sea. It was bumpy, and in a sense, you could say I failed my way up in some cases.

A person who does not know life and only knows what they are told by people of a certain mindset may feel that it's a sin to learn through trial and error. Trial and error are a very common way to learn, as unfortunate as that is. It may seem in some ways a great teacher. No one wants to fall in love with someone who uses trial and error moments with their heart, but it's inevitable at times that someone must go through it. My journey has kept me rooted in reality. It's no coincidence that I work in reality TV.

In my case, there was a time when many people judged the choices I made without understanding my reasoning. In a supernatural way, I think that was meant for me to experience. I think that experience was tailored by God. In life you must sink or swim, and as a man if you crumble because your feelings are hurt, then your chances of survival are slim. As a Black man, every stage of my journey required deep thought, even when I made simple decisions like what neighborhood to stop in to get gas. Risk analysis is a 24-hour lifetime job for us. It takes a toll on you. For those who find it hard to do well under this type of constant pressure, they usually end up as a statistic, and those of us who make it work do not recognize until later that we are living in survival mode and probably suffering from some level of PTSD. Our lives are filled with physical and emotional challenges. The emotional challenges hurt the worst because they ultimately do the most damage. Emotional stress affects the decisions we make. I recall many of my friends being smart guys who lacked confidence in their ability to do something constructive. They felt that they would not be accepted by White people.

Our schools show us a host of successful White people, afterward we learn of successful Blacks who were disrespected and always looking for approval as well as acceptance by their White counterparts. Teaching our history that way does not incite a powerful feeling in us, especially in the modern-day climate. The issue many of us face daily is enough to kill any joy. I'm talking about just having the surface level of understanding. The more I found out about the traps we face as we struggle daily from being poor, as well as the systematic and political traps made for us, the more I realized that it was mandatory that I find a way to survive and then thrive. I could not afford to pity myself while on my journey; the moments I did, yielded no benefits other than the reminder that after I was done sulking, I had to get up and do the work. The world does not care about my feelings. That is something I like to tell people, to give them a real-life perspective. Family and close friends may care about your feelings in certain circumstances, but if they care too much, they are on the verge of enabling you. This is of course circumstantial. Now when I say the world doesn't care, what I mean is that once you walk outside your house, you step into an arena where everyone is looking for results, an ROI, a way out. Everyone wants something, and that something is a priority. So, cry all you want, frown, stomp, but at the end of your tantrum do the work. Doing the work is where you build your skills. In most cases it takes repetitions to become great. I remember when I first heard someone admit that they failed their way to the top. I was surprised that anyone would let that come out of their mouth in front of anyone who was not a close friend. I had been looking at failure the wrong way for a long time. When a person admits they failed their way up they were saying all they did was keep trying to do a thing until they got it. Now the difference between me and them is that in the world we live I would need a lighter shade of skin to be allotted to get my reps in while on the job without being let go. I was introduced to the working world knowing that I had to work ten times harder than others because I'm a Black person, a Black man.

Although I have never liked accepting that, I use it as a guideline for myself. For a long while and somewhat today I have insecure moments regarding my education. Most of my education came from life experience and whatever things I was curious enough to teach myself. There are times I am in a group setting and people are discussing concepts or parts of history that they learned through traditional education and it's those times where I find myself saying less and trying to understand what I missed. The good thing is this is the information age, I'm a quick learner, and there is Google so what I didn't know is easy to find out. It's my creed to stay strong and adjust on the fly.

When I say it, I say it with passion, because I need them to understand that it's true when people say only the strong survive. Currently in life and in certain industries I do see where people are becoming more concerned with other people's feelings, but as for Blacks, we experience blatant disrespect at all levels and industries. We must be strong and not allow our emotions to get the best of us because that is when our thinking is not clear.

Doing the work is my principle. I believe that when I do what needs to be done to achieve my goal, the reward is mine; it's a part of who I am, and no one can take that away from me. The great thing about my career field is that there are great rewards when you do the work. There is always something to learn and more than one way to do a job. Because I take much pride in my work, I have been guilty of expecting things to be done my way. However, I discovered, as a leader it is important to uplift my co-workers. Trusting them to get the job done is one way to accomplish that. There is a hierarchy, and everyone matters in their respective places. Trust allows a person to strive for growth. To me, that has been my life, so I appreciate the challenges and the rewards.

My journey did not make sense to me. While in the process it seemed like I was all over the place. Every time I left town, I thought I was leaving a bad situation and running to a good situation. When I made it to my destination, I was starting all over again. Each time I settled into a new state I had a plan to build from that. In my head I was going to change my life completely around in a short amount of time. What I found was that everything I was doing started to connect. I was being prepared for my future. I didn't see it that way. For some reason I was mentally stuck in time. In my head I was a young boy who just wanted attention. I was stuck in place, and life was moving all around me. On the outside I often portrayed that I knew what I was doing, even if I messed up. On the inside, I felt the emptiness interfere, but I knew that I could not intentionally allow anyone to see where I was lacking. I did not realize how immature I was. I had limited knowledge; but growth occurred through my responsibilities and thoughts, but sometimes my abilities were elementary. Although I was able to get information from someone and immediately apply what I was missing, it took time and effort to store something and see it to fruition. I understood the harsh realities of life, I lacked the correct principles that would allow me to execute my endeavors. I did things I thought I was supposed to do. When you're in survival mode, you can be very narrow-minded.

Life is a very unpredictable journey, as you can see through my story. I stress how important it is to obtain skills and principles to live by. You never know what you are going to need and when you will need it. I was clearly learning a lot of things on the fly, but the reality is that was the way that part of my journey went. Honestly, looking back, I found a silver lining in some of the things I thought were grave mistakes. Had I not quit college in Minneapolis and moved back to St. Louis, I would not be here today, doing what I love. Operating out of fear and misunderstanding took me on a path I thought was never ending. Looking back, I realize even more now because the way my mindset was at the time I was just trying to survive, and when things did not go as planned, I felt like my whole world was falling apart. That was evidence of my immaturity. I was impatient with myself, and I felt like a complete failure for a long time.

One truth about life, regardless of who you are, you will have good and bad experiences that contribute to shaping your identity. Every situation offers guidance, and I truly believe that based on the energy and outlook you have on what's going on, things will ultimately turn out that way. If there is one overall message, I want you to take away from this book, it is this: look at things the way they are and not how you think they are supposed to be. Seeing things in their reality will help you come up with the best solution to the problem. Once you understand your truth and plan, tap into your faith and work, and then expect to see those unseen things that you are anticipating in your spirit, to manifest. That is how I made things better for myself. I mixed my truth and my faith together. This approach helped me understand, as each day passed, my perspective. Making a choice to believe that God was going to aid me as I moved with good intentions was empowering. Every step I took in the right direction added up, and eventually I was living in a whole new world with a renewed mind. If you are starting from a low place, a renewed mind is a great goal to put at the top of your list. Once your mind changes, life follows. You won't know everything that is coming to you, but you will recognize a difference in the way you see things.

While writing this book, moments unfolded as I shared my story, and my mind began racing. It was not an easy task for me. First, I had to catch myself in the middle of re-experiencing some of the things I wrote about. Secondly, I had to decide what parts of my story could be told without doing any damage to anyone else. Lastly, which turned out to be the hardest part for me, I came to the realization that some people who were in my life at certain times meant me no good. Writing this book, I figured out that I am pretty good at forgiving and pushing things to the back of my mind. After all, I come from a forgiving people.

I feel like that will get in the way of what it is I must do. I think my next phase in life is to open my eyes even more by going to therapy. Yes, therapy. I encourage all Black people who feel the need to express their frustrations, angst, any emotion, to find a therapist and go, talk about whatever you need to talk about.

Ninety percent of the time I feel like I'm good, but there are moments I feel heavy pressure in my head, and I think it is because I've never dealt with my childhood trauma. Honestly, I did not know it was something I should address until I began to see more people on the social media platform talking about it. There is so much more to my story, some things I left out because I am still in the process of living those situations. Based on the life I live today I am very optimistic, and I expect that in the end of it all I will have lived an awesome life. That will be my final testament of faith in God.

www.ingramcontent.com/pod-product-compliance
Lightning Source LLC
Chambersburg PA
CBHW071454070526
44578CB00001B/332